Crochet
FOR
BEGINNERS

A Step by Step Illustrated Instruction Guide for Beginners with 10 Easy Patterns

By Lily Chester

© **Copyright 2023 — All rights reserved.**

The content contained within this book may not be reproduced, duplicated, or transmitted without direct written permission from the author or the publisher.

Under no circumstances will any blame or legal responsibility be held against the publisher, or author, for any damages, reparation, or monetary loss due to the information contained within this book. Either directly or indirectly.

Legal Notice:

This book is copyright protected. This book is only for personal use. You cannot amend, distribute, sell, use, quote or paraphrase any part, or the content within this book, without the consent of the author or publisher.

Disclaimer Notice:

Please note the information contained within this document is for educational and entertainment purposes only. All effort has been executed to present accurate, up-to-date, and reliable, complete information. No warranties of any kind are declared or implied. Readers acknowledge that the author is not engaging in the rendering of legal, financial, medical, or professional advice. The content within this book has been derived from various sources. Please consult a licensed professional before attempting any techniques outlined in this book.

By reading this document, the reader agrees that under no circumstances is the author responsible for any losses, direct or indirect, which are incurred as a result of the use of the information contained within this document, including, but not limited to, — errors, omissions, or inaccuracies.

Table of Contest

Introduction 7

Chapter 1: Your Basic Crocheting Knowledge 9

    What is Crochet? 9

    What Can You Make with Crochet? 10

    Difference between Knitting and Crochet 10

    Reasons Crochet Can Be the Perfect Hobby 11

    What You Need to Get Started 12

    Crochet Hooks 12

    How to Hold Your Hook the Right Way? 16

    Yarn 18

    Stitch Markers 19

    Scissors 21

    Swatch Ruler and Needle/ Hook Gauge 22

    Tapestry Needles 23

    Flexible Measuring Tape 24

    Project Bag 24

    Row Counter 25

    Yarn Swift and Ball Winder 26

    Pom-Pom Maker 28

    Finish It Up with Blocking 29

Chapter 2: Your Crochet How-Tos............................ 33
How to Hold Your Yarn and Hook?........................ 33
Know the Right and Wrong Side of Your Fabric................ 35
How Do You Tell the Right Side Of A Crochet Project?.......... 36

Chapter 3: Variations and Finishing........................ 61
Variations in Stitches.. 61

Chapter 4: Save Yourself from Making These Newbie Mistakes...... 75
Stitch Your Hook in the Wrong Chain When Starting a Project.... 76
Starting Loops with Linked Chain Instead of a Magic Loop....... 76
Use the Same Sized Hook for Your Chain as You Use For the Entire Project................................ 77
Shrinking or Growing Crochet............................. 77
Trusting the Manufacturers' Knots......................... 78
Not Knowing About Yarn Quality.......................... 78
Not Knowing About C2C.................................. 79
Not Knowing How to Crochet in Rounds.................... 79
Not Knowing How to Weave in Ends the Right Way........... 80
Not Counting Your Rows................................. 81
Not Counting the Starting Chain Correctly or Where to Put the First Stitch.......................... 81
Not Leaving the Yarn Tail Long Enough..................... 82

Chapter 5: Types of Crochet You Will See in the World........... 83
Amigurumi Crochet..................................... 83
Aran Crochet... 84
Bavarian Crochet....................................... 85
Bullion Crochet... 86
Broomstick Crochet..................................... 87
Bruges Crochet... 88
Clothesline Crochet..................................... 89
Clones Lace Crochet.................................... 90

Cro-Hook Crochet 91

Filet Crochet. 92

Finger Crochet 93

Freeform Crochet 94

Hairpin Crochet 95

Micro Crochet 97

Overlay Crochet 98

Pineapple Crochet. 99

Stained Glass Crochet 100

Symbol Crochet 101

Tapestry Crochet. 102

Tunisian Crochet 103

Chapter 6: Let's Start Crocheting! 105

Beginners Crochet Washcloths 106

Beginners Crochet Scarf 108

Bobble Headband. 109

Classic Granny Squares. 111

Beanie. 114

Scrunchie 116

Baby Blanket. 117

Ear Warmers 119

Crochet Pillow Cover 121

Crochet Sweater 123

Conclusion 127

References 129

Introduction

Crochet is an ancient craft that has been enjoyed by people of all ages and backgrounds for centuries. It is a versatile art form that allows you to create a wide range of items, from blankets and sweaters to delicate lace doilies and intricate amigurumi figures. If you have always been curious about crochet but never knew where to start, this book is for you. In this book "Crochet for Beginners, you will be guided step by step through the basics of this beautiful craft. It starts by explaining what crochet is and how it differs from other forms of needlework, such as knitting and embroidery. It will also cover the tools and materials you will need to get started, including different types of hooks, yarns, and accessories.

Once you have your materials in hand, you will be guided through the essential crochet techniques, including how to hold your hook and yarn, make basic stitches such as chains, single crochets, and double crochets, and read a crochet pattern. This book will also cover more advanced techniques, such as crocheting in the round, increasing and decreasing stitches, and creating different textures with different stitch patterns. You will also learn about different stitch variations that will come in handy in your future crochet project to help give them more accent and texture. This book also discusses the mistakes beginners often make while crocheting and how you can save yourself from making them by following some tips and tricks. As you progress through the book, you will be introduced to a variety of beginner-friendly projects that will help you practice your new skills. These projects are beginner friendly and will give you lots to practice your crocheting skill on. Each project includes step-by-step instructions to help you follow along.

However, crochet is more than just a technical skill. It's also a creative outlet that allows you to express yourself in unique and beautiful ways. Throughout the book, you will be provided with tips and advice on choosing the right yarn and colors for your projects and combining different stitch patterns to create interesting textures. This book is perfect for learning crocheting on your own or in a group because crochet is a social activity that helps you relax and ease your way out through stressful times in life. By the end of this book, you will have the skills and confidence to start creating your own beautiful crochet projects. But more than that, you will have discovered a new hobby that can bring you joy, relaxation, and a sense of accomplishment for years to come. So whether you are looking for a way to unwind after a long day or a new creative challenge, we invite you to join us on this exciting journey into the world of crochet.

Chapter 1: Your Basic Crocheting Knowledge

Have you ever seen someone crocheting and wondered how hard that must be? Or maybe you wanted to try crochet but did not know how to start it? This chapter will teach you all the basic knowledge you need about crochet — what crochet is, why people of all ages are crazy about this craft, and some terms that only crochet experts know.

Crochet is a form of craft that involves looping or hooking a piece of yarn with the help of a single hook made from wood, metal, or bone. Unlike weaving or knitting, it is a more recent fiber art method. Different crochet techniques, such as the Irish crocheting style, involve distinctive designs and motifs. It is well-known and is very different from knitting, which requires open stitches. Crochet requires you to close the stitch before moving on to the next one.

What is Crochet?

Crochet is a type of needlework you use to create fabric by looping yarn using a hook. There are many different variations of crochet present nowadays. However, no one is exactly sure how and where this contagious craft started. The crochet that we are familiar with today was spread in Europe in the 1800s and has gained popularity throughout the years!

What Can You Make with Crochet?

Crochet is one of the most versatile crafts you can use to create various items. Popular crochet items include blankets, scarves, key chains, and dishcloths. These are just the "popular" items you will find everywhere. However, just like I mentioned earlier, you can make about anything you can imagine using different crochet techniques due to its versatility.

Difference between Knitting and Crochet

People often confuse knitting with crochet as both of these crafts revolve around looping using a piece of yarn and hooks. However, crochet is very different from knitting or weaving. Let's see how these two are different from each other:

- *Less time-consuming:* Crochet uses a single hook that makes it faster than knitting, which requires two hooks to loop or weaves the yarn together. Knitting is a continuous chain of loops, while with crochet, you have to close the loop before moving on.
- *More versatile:* Unlike knitting, which can only be done using yarn, you can crochet using any kind of thread or string. This makes crochet fabric less stretchy than knit fabric.
- *More creativity:* With knit fabric, you can only make clothes, while crocheting gives you the option of making anything from home décor items to garments to accessories such as bracelets, bags, and key chains.
- *Redo mistakes easily:* Crochet uses one live stitch, making it less likely to unravel accidentally than knitting. To fix any mistakes, you only need to rip back a few stitches and do it again until you get the desired result. Easy peasy, right?!

While both crafts are addicting and beautiful in their own ways, people often refer to crochet as being easier than knitting. It all comes down to what you want to do.

Reasons Crochet Can Be the Perfect Hobby

There are a gazillion reasons I can tell you that makes crocheting worth spending time and money on; however, among the many things, newcomers are attracted to include its health advantages. The therapeutic effects of crocheting are well-known, including tactile pleasure, rhythmic nature, and social connections. There are many ways crocheting helps us in achieving better health. Some fun facts that make it the healthiest hobby include:

- *Say goodbye to stress and Anxiety:* With the fast-paced life we are living these days, it is no surprise that our daily lives are filled with anxiety and stress trying to keep up with the racing world. Crocheting helps divert our attention from all those stressful things by switching focus on the creative process and giving us a much-needed break to catch our breath. It calms our nervous notions and feelings by concentrating on the repetitive actions involved in making the individual stitches and counting rows.
- *Ease your way to mental peace:* Through crocheting, your mind is transformed into a kind of awareness that is closer to meditation by continuous and repeated sewing. You can get all the benefits of conventional meditation through crochet. If you have a hard time following proper meditation, then try using crocheting as a pre-meditation practice.
- *No more procrastination:* The sense of success from completing a long and hard project helps you stay motivated at work, college, or home. Crocheting is a versatile craft that gives you a lot of options to make your desired item and never get bored. The result can be a gift for you or someone else that gives you a fantastic feeling of productivity.
- *Fuel up on dopamine:* Your body releases dopamine whenever you do something enjoyable or fun. This neurotransmitter acts as a natural antidepressant by influencing your overall mood. Hobbies such as crocheting can help improve our moods and self-esteem.

- *Perfect Social Activity:* Crocheting is one of the most commonly related activities that can be done in a group as well as alone. You can find many platforms that host a crocheting gathering to finish big projects together that helps improve your social connection and decrease your chances of developing social anxiety.

What You Need to Get Started

The material used for crochet can be hard to find because of the many different kinds of hooks, yarns, and fibers available in the markets nowadays. Some people prefer handmade or pre-made items that work for their particular needs. It is up to you what material you wish to go for when it comes to the tools used for crocheting. The basic things you would need are a crochet hook and some yarn. However, to make things easier, many items are available in the market to help you save time and get crocheting faster. Supplies such as stitch markers, crochet needles, Swatch rulers, crochet scissors, row counters, and so on are additional necessities that will help you in doing your projects easily and accurately. Learning about each individual tool and supply will help you better understand what to look for when you start your crocheting journey.

Crochet Hooks

A crochet hook is one of the essential tools used for crochet. You cannot crochet anything without a hook as it serves the same purpose as knitting needles; however, unlike knitting needles, there is a hook on the end of the shaft, and you only need one to crochet. The hook is used to pull the yarn through the created loops along the handle; this allows you to make an array of crochet stitches at a time. Although it seems simple, it can become complicated if you do not know which hook to use for your specific project. Let us learn about different types of hooks and get you hooked on this craft!

Types Of Crochet Hooks

Two commonly found crochet hook types are used by beginners at the start of their crochet journey. The inline and tapered hooks may look similar on the surface, but they have subtle differences that might affect how you crochet.

Inline Crochet Hooks:

Just as the name refers, their hook is the same width as the shaft and has an angular appearance with a defined point at the lip and a deeper mouth compared to other hooks. The sharper angles make this hook helpful in creating tighter uniform stitches which makes it perfect for crocheting projects such as scarves and gloves.

Tapered Crochet Hooks:

These hooks have a lip that extends slightly beyond the shaft width and has a rounder head with a shallower mouth than their inline counterparts. The rounded features of this hook make it perfect for making quick and easy projects such as blankets. This tapered hook minimizes the frequency of you splitting your yarn with your horn mid-project.

Although these two are the most basic crochet hooks recommended for beginners, you can explore many different types of crochet hooks in the markets. Some other crochet hook types are:

- *Tunisian Crochet Hooks:* These hooks are longer than your traditional hooks and often include a stopper at the end. This helps you keep all your stitches on the hook as you work through the project and is similar to knitting. Some very specific projects use the Tunisian stitch technique. For example, the dense fabric made using this technique makes it ideal for warm and thick items such as blankets, scarves, and dishcloths.
- *Ergonomic Crochet Hooks:* Sleek like a jaguar, these hooks come in either inline or tapered styles, but feature larger handles designed to reduce wrist soreness from extended crocheting. You can also find ergonomic handles that easily slip on and off your favorite regular hooks.

- *Knook Crochet Hooks:* In these hooks, the tail end of the shaft has an eye that is used to thread through a nylon cord and move your stitches on the cord to create knit-like stitches. These are specifically used for projects that replicate knitting. Advanced crocheters use these hooks for complicated projects.

Crochet Hook Materials:

Just like many other crafting tools, crochet hooks come in a variety of different materials. Choosing the material is based on how it will react to the yarn fiber you are using.

- Wooden hooks: Crochet hooks made of wood are less slippery than other materials and tend to have higher friction. This makes great for preventing the yarn from slipping over the hook shaft. However, it can make it hard to finish stitches and make the work slower.
- Bamboo hooks: Just like wooden hooks, these also have the same benefits and disadvantages. However, with time and use, their friction will lessen, which will allow beginners to slowly increase their speed with experience.
- Plastic Hooks: Plastic tends to have no friction, which is great for fast and experienced crocheters. However, due to the quality, they may have some imperfections in their molds which will cause the yarn to get stuck and fray. Also, plastic hooks tend to break more easily with continued use because they are far more pliable.
- Steel Hooks: Steel is one of the strongest and most durable materials, so you will never have to worry about them bending or breaking easily. Steel crochet hooks are often used for making thread crochet. The most traditional crochet hooks are also made from steel. However, due to the hardness of the material, metal hooks can strain your hand faster and can make it harder to finish long and big projects.

- Aluminum Hooks: This is the most widely available crochet hook material. You can easily find the right-sized crochet hook in this material, and they are often sold in sets at very reasonable prices. They have low friction; however, they can also cause your hand to strain, much like steel crochet hooks.

Labeling a Crochet Hook:

A crochet hook has different parts. Looking at the picture above, you can see there are five parts of a crochet hook. Let's see what each one is used for from the top.

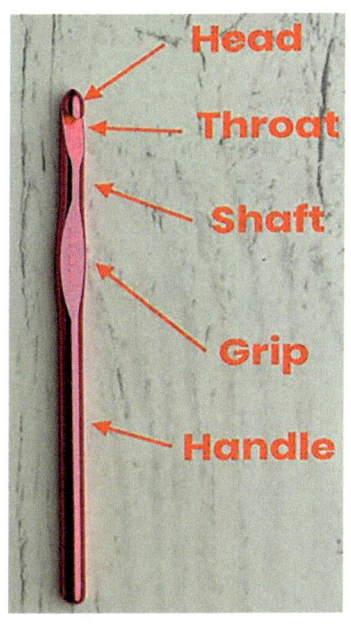

- *The Head:* This is the main part of the hook that consists of the nose or lip of the hook and mouth, which is used to pull the yarn through the loops or stitches.
- *The Throat:* This part starts right from the mouth and widens to help keep the yarn in place while looping or stitching.
- *The Shaft:* This is the part where you would loop the yarn over the hook and the first place where the hook reaches its maximum diameter.
- *The Grip:* Also known as the thumb rest, it is a small indentation that allows you to manipulate the hook with your thumb and index finger while providing some comfort while holding the hook.
- *The Handle:* As the name states, this is the part that extends to the crocheter's hand, providing support; it extends beyond the thumb rest.

Hook Sizes:

The size of a crochet hook refers to the diameter of the shaft. The larger the shaft diameter, the larger your stitches will be. This will affect the size of your final product, so make sure you pick the right hook size for your project. Whatever yarn you choose, the label will tell you exactly what hook size you should use, along with what sized gauge you need. A gauge is the number of crochet stitches you need to make per inch to ensure that your tension is correct when doing a project to get the finished look as intended. The yarn gauge and recommended hook sizes can be represented as symbols on the yarn label, as in the example below.

How to Hold Your Hook the Right Way?

There is no right or wrong when it comes to holding a crochet hook. The right way is the way you feel most comfortable holding it. However, two traditional grips can help you get started.

The Knife Grip:

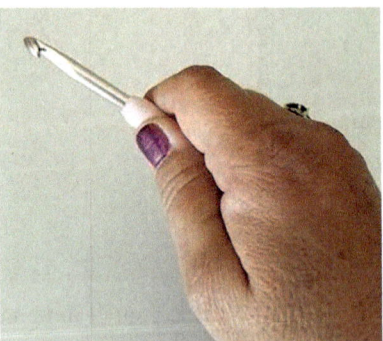

As shown in the picture above, a knife grip is like holding a knife to cut a steak, except you are using yarn instead of food. You keep the handle in the palm of your hand while your thumb and index finger stay close to the hook. By placing your thumb in the thumb rest, you will have a lot of control over your work.

The Pencil Grip:

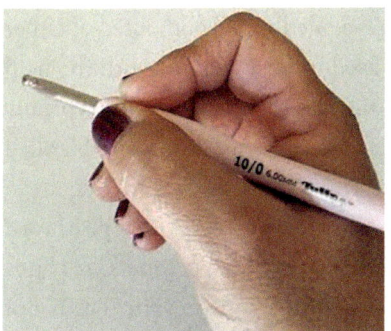

Imagine holding a pencil while taking your SAT test. Yep, that's the right way! With this grip, the end of the handle is to the back of your hand, and you use a downward motion to create stitches. It is the reverse of the knife grip but just as effective. It all depends on what you feel comfortable with!

Choose the Right Hook

There are many things to look for when choosing a hook; it can be very confusing. But do not fear. I have just the checklist for you to consider when choosing your favorite hook:

- *How comfortable is it?* The most important factor in choosing any craft as a hobby is ensuring you feel comfortable doing it. Your body might not feel as relaxed if you choose tools that will strain it. Try testing different hook materials and stick with what feels the best in your hands!
- *Does it match the pattern I am going for?* When starting a project, you will see a suggestion list will the hook size and yarn weight for a specific pattern. These are the only suggestions; you can always give it a personal touch and switch up the pattern by choosing a thinner or chunkier yarn and hook size.
- *Can it match the yarn I chose?* Whatever yarn you choose, you will see a suggested hook size on the label. Always make sure that your hook size and yarn match because you do not want to use a small hook for bulky weight yarn, as it will make things worse. So, switch your yarn and hook size at the same time.

Yarn

Considering the definition, yarn is a piled strand composed of either man-made or natural fibers and is used to form a fabric with the help of techniques such as weaving or knitting. A crochet yarn is typically made from a very fine cotton thread which is used to make blanked and other heirloom projects. However, the choice of crochet yarn can vary by person and type of project they are going for. The type of yarn you choose can impact the finished project. For beginners, it is important to consider simple and less artificially made yarn that is not too heavy nor too light. Millions of yarn brands, colors, and textures are available in the market. And honestly, some are too pretty to give up! I have been through that dilemma; however, considering the lack of experience, you should always start with basic cotton yarn with medium weight for your initial practice project. As you gain experience, there is no limit to the possibilities when it comes to choosing yarn for more complex projects! The best way to choose your first yarn is to consider the weight, fiber content, and price. In my opinion, a level 4 standard yarn is perfect for beginners. It is called a worsted or bulky weight yarn, also known as a chunky yarn, that is smooth and light in color. The best material would be anywhere from wool, premium acrylic, or a blended one. And the price is usually up to you on how much you are comfortable spending on it. The market is full of different price options, so choose the one that fits your pocket!

Stitch Markers

These small hooks are visual and tangible reminders of something in your crochet project. These are a crocheter's best friends after a crochet hook and yarn, as these will help you finish your work more accurately and nicely. You will find many different kinds of stitch markers in the market, some fancy, some shiny, and some plain gaudy; however, not all of them are meant for crocheting. We all want cute-looking markers on our project but trust me, these will complicate your work. Stitch markers used for crochet can be opened and closed as they are attached to any stitches and removed when they are not needed anymore. There are two different types of stitch markers used in the crochet project.

- Open ring:

Also known as closed stitch markers or O-ring markers, these can be made of anything from plastic, rubber, metal, or anything. Closed markers are often made of wires which are great for larger needle sizes.

- Split ring markers:

Also known as the open stitch markers, which can be split into three further types:

- Clasp markers: made with lobster claw clasps like the ones we use on necklaces and bracelets.

- Clip markers: These can be clipped like safety pins.
- Split ring markers: just like paper clips, these markers can be split open.

Where Can You Use Stitch Markers in Crochet?

Stitch markers can help crocheting when you are in a stitch. They are not just meant to mark the back or front of a project, and if used correctly, they can help bring more accuracy to your project. A few ways you can use stitch markers when crocheting are:

- Mark those rounds: A frequent problem that many crocheters face when making rounds for a stuffed animal, a hat, or a bag, is that we forget the spot for the start and end of the round. And oftentimes, you would not even realize that you missed stitch count, and suddenly the tiny koala has a crooked arm. Try using a stitch marked from the end of the third round and onwards, insert the marker into the last loop of your previously done round, and lock and move it up every two rounds.
- Mark those patterns: Crocheting is fun due to the variety of stitches you can do in it, from lace stitch to a pentagon-shaped granny square. Try using a stitch marker at the beginning and end of your repeated pattern. This will help you concentrate on your beautiful project, and you can easily add other colored markers to mark the other important spots in the pattern, such as the increases and decreases. Crochet markers are just what you need when you are working on a big project that takes longer, so you will remember what exactly you were doing till the end of the project.
- Mark those mistakes: Stitch markers are the perfect gift for your crochet mistakes. Even the most experienced crocheter will make errors with a new pattern every once in a while. So why panic when you can just calmly mark the error and move on? One of the things I love about crochet is that you

do not have to unravel the entire project for every mistake; of course, not all mistakes can be fixed. However, you can always mark a missed stitch at the end of a row or that square that turned out to be a pyramid. Just mark those mistakes for now and decide later what you want to do with them. Simple right? Although sometimes you might just have to redo the whole thing, trust me, we have all been there!

- Mark those stitch counts: How many times have you had to repeatedly count those stitches with frustration? Stitch markers can help you divide the row into pieces, so you do not have to count stitches every time. All you have to do is hang a marker on the first and then after every ten or fifteen stitches. This way, you will get an idea of where you are just from a short glance at those colorful markers. You can even use a different colored marker to pinpoint the end of your row because those edges can be really tricky.
- Mark those loops: The one thing I love about crochet is how convenient it is to travel with your work in progress or even work on several projects simultaneously using a single hook. You can use a lockable stitch marker to help secure the loop left in your unfinished project and work on it later on or whenever you feel like it. Even if your kid pulls on the yarn, your work is not going anywhere!

Scissors

Like other crochet materials, scissors are also all about your own personal preference. I personally like to keep tiny sewing scissors in my crochet bag to cut any loose or extra piece of yarn. If you are always on the go, you can get small foldable pair of scissors or even a regular pair of nail clippers that is sharp enough to cut a piece of yarn. Nowadays, you can find various varieties of scissors with different features used for different crafts. You can buy small, capped scissors to protect your project if you like to keep your project along with your other supplies in the same bag. Any kind of scissors can be used as crochet scissors; you just have to find whatever you are comfortable using and putting into your crochet bag. However, make sure to tell the rest of your family that these are for crochet use only!

Swatch Ruler and Needle/ Hook Gauge

Are you worried about all the counting and math it requires when crocheting anything? Does it kill all the fun out of a craft for you? Then a Swatch ruler and needle hook gauge is just the right tool to have in your crochet supplies. It is a multipurpose tool that does all the crocheting math for you. It helps you to accurately determine the stitch and row gauge and ensures you are using the correct size crochet hook for corrections. The Swatch ruler part of this tool helps you isolate a section of your work to easily count both the stitches and rows. Every crocheting class will tell you how to use this fantastic tool in the beginning, so you know how important it is to always have one in your bag!

Tapestry Needles

These are essential for when you are finishing up your project. A tapestry needle is a small pin-like needle tool used to weave in the leftover yarn tails on a project and seam together crochet pieces. For example, suppose you are working on a crocheted baby blanket or even a crochet hat. In that case, you will need tapestry needles to help tie in those loose edges of your project or combine together different crochet pieces. You will find a variety of tapestry needles in craft stores everywhere. They come in sets that are available in small travel-sized cases to help you conveniently carry them in your crochet bag. Tapestry needles are made from metal or plastic and can have a straight or bent tip. The bent tip needles are easier to get into the crochet stitches and help you bury or weave the ends. While the plastic finishing needles are useful when you have a short yarn tail on a project, as they can easily work through the stitches with the small yarn tail inside.

Flexible Measuring Tape

Flexible tape measures are essential tools for any craft. Whether it is knitting, stitching, or crocheting. These come in a variety of lengths and types, so you can choose the one you are comfortable with. The retractable is one of my favorites because it does not take up a lot of space in your crochet bag and does not tangle up in your project. How frustrating can that be? It is handy when you want to measure the size of any large project, such as a shawl or blanket. Tape measures are like big flexible scales made from soft plastic material with numbers on top measuring both inches and centimeters. It can be stretched out, so before using any flexible tape measure, measure it against a ruler occasionally that will help you measure your project requirements correctly. Like other crochet notions, finding the tape that works for you is all about personal preference!

Project Bag

A project or crochet bag is your lifesaver when keeping your project and crafting materials safe. Although some people prefer using a regular large-sized Ziploc bag to keep their projects separate, it is difficult to carry around and be seen holding a giant Ziploc bag with crocheted yarn inside. It looks cheap and makes your project look weird, all crumbled inside a plastic bag. Project bags are trendy, and there are a variety of different kinds and colors; you can even get one customized just for you! These are perfect for keeping your works in progress along with your favorite hook and other supplies inside, and take it with you on the go wherever you want. So make sure to put this on your list of crochet supplies to get a trendy, adorable, and whimsical project bag for your crochet work and other supplies. There are many ways to get your desired project bag: make your own, get one from knitting conventions, stalk your favorite designers at sheep and wool festivals, or snatch your favorite one whenever they have a shop update. Project bags are reusable; however, it is also essential to have multiple project bags at hand for when you have multiple WIPs (works in progress) to ensure all your projects are safe and sound until you have the time to finish them! Choosing the right bag is all about your preference, so keep looking until you find the one you love!

Row Counter

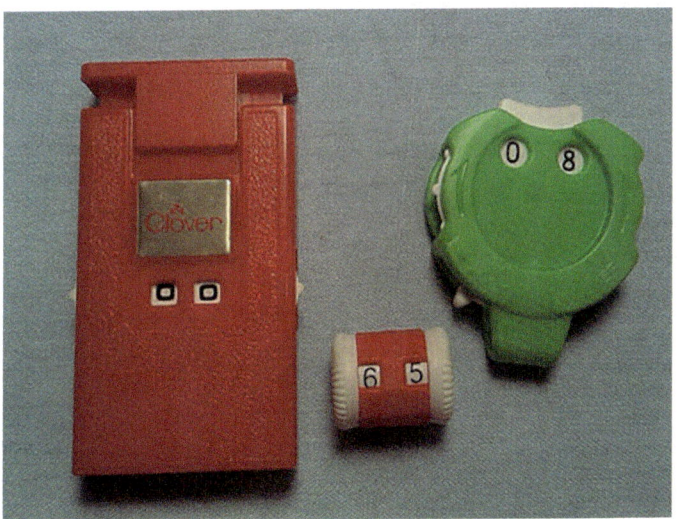

When working on complicated patterns, it can be frustrating to stop and count the number of rows you have done and how many you need to do. Imagine stopping every few minutes to write down where you are, how many rows you need to do before making a round, and so on. It can interrupt your workflow and really kill the fun out of crocheting. For times like these, there is a tool called a row counter which you can use to count and track your rows, rounds, or stitches. It is a tiny, lightweight, simple device with a push-button operation that can easily fit into the palm of your hand. You easily loop a thread or elastic through a hole at the side and wear it around your neck as a necklace while crocheting. It will be easier to access and make your work a lot easier. You can use a row counter for various reasons, including counting rows, rounds, pattern repeats, or shaping. Although it is recommended to use the simple and manual row counter for beginners, many different kinds of row counters are available. You can find digital counters, dial row counters, decorative counters, and an application you can use on your smartphone as counters. Like any other crochet supply, it all comes down to your preference and requirements.

Yarn Swift and Ball Winder

How many times have you tried to make anything out of yarn and ended up getting all the yarn tangled up? A yarn swifter is a device specifically made to hold an untwisted hank of yarn and rotate it in circles, turning it into a ball. Any sized hank of yarn can fit into it due to its adjustable center that expands and detracts the diameter of the device. The swift works well with the assistance of another piece called a ball winder. Although it does not fall under the necessity list of crochet supplies, it can help if you plan to make crochet your everyday hobby.

What is the purpose of the swift, and do you really need it?

When I first came across this device, I did not understand the exact need for it for my crochet passion. However, after searching for tutorials on how it is used, I discovered that the main purpose of it is to prevent the yarn from tangling when you wind the yarn into a ball. Now what is a hank of yarn, you ask? It is a twisted ring of a yard that is looped together to form a big circle. Most yarns are sold in the shape of a yank. The first you do when you start crocheting anything is that you unwind the yank into a ball, so the fibers do not rub together and become a tangled mess. It would make you hate crocheting if you had to repeatedly fix the tangles while you worked on your project. This is why having a swift at hand will help create less mess while crocheting. A yarn swift is best if used in conjunction with a ball winder. Both combined together can make unwinding yarn a piece of cake. Having a swift around is a personal choice; if you do not want to tackle a hank of yarn for hours before starting a project, get a swift. It all depends on your preference and what you are comfortable with while crocheting.

How does a yarn swift even work?

There are wide varieties of the yarn swift with different shapes and sizes; however, the basic mechanism is the same in all of them. The process starts with setting up the swift on a tabletop or a surface; once the swift is set and sturdy, expand the swift to a circumference according to the hank of yarn you are using. Ensure the swift is slightly smaller than the hank to make it easier to work with. Once your swift is assembled correctly, open up a hank of yarn by untwisting the middle loop; gently place it onto the swift, ensure it fits the circumference, and lock it into place. You can use a ball winder or manually wind the yarn string into a ball while the swift rotates in a circle to unwind the yarn. And voila, you are left with a beautifully winded yarn ball ready for crocheting!

Pom-Pom Maker

Pom poms are fun to add a cheerful look to your crochet project. You can easily use them to give soft and fluffy embellishments to your hats, blankets, pillows, etc. Many projects can be made using only pom poms, like beautiful pom-pom carpets, wall hanging, garlands, wreaths, or fluffy jewelry. Pom-pom making can be an easy and addictive craft.

It takes minutes to make a pom-pom using a pom-pom maker. A tool I am fond of these days is called the clover pom-pom maker, which makes pom-pom making even more fun! It comes in 7 different sizes, from extra small, to extra-large; you can make pom poms of all sizes. All you need is some yarn, scissors, and pom-pom maker.

How to make pom-pom using the pom pom maker tool?

Start off by choosing the right size for your project. The pom-pom maker has two sides that look like arches joined in the middle. Open a one-sided arch and align its halves which are located side by side. Now wrap the yarn around the arch and pinch the loose end with the hand facing outwards. You should be able to cover the entire arch by going back and forth a couple of times. Ensure you are keeping a uniform tension to ensure the arch is even. After you finish the first arch, pull the strand between the gap and start wrapping the second arch the same way. Once you are done wrapping the second arch, cut the yarn when it's facing the outward side of the arch. Then take your scissors and place them in the gap of the first arch, then cut all around, including the stand between the two arches. Lastly, cut a long strand of yarn, wrap it around the ridge a couple of times, and tie it tightly with a few knots to secure your pom pom. Now open the arches and pull the two pieces apart, and viola, your pom-pom is done!

Finish It Up with Blocking

The final step of crocheting is blocking. It is something that almost every crocheter has heard of; however, only a few of them actually do it. Blocking is a finishing process of stretching, shaping, or wetting a finished project to help even out the stitches and set the final size. This helps smooth out your project and give it a professional look, as yarn fibers have a natural "springiness" to them. Blocking helps expand and then settle it to the shape and size it is pinned to. It is essential in helping to fill up any gaps in the stitches, preventing the fabric from curling, and creating an even and finished look for the project.

Types of Blocking:

Blocking can be done using different methods; almost all of them follow a basic method; however, some use different materials:
- *Steam blocking:* In this method, you apply steam to your crochet fabric using a garment steamer or iron.

- *Spray blocking:* It is a simple blocking method that uses spray water filled with water and washed wool detergent. You start by pinning your fabric on a blocking board, then spray it with warm water and allow it to air dry thoroughly.
- *Wet blocking:* This is the most common method of blocking in which you soak the fabric in warm soaped water and press out the excess water. Then you pin the wet fabric onto a blocking board and allow it to air dry on its own. This is usually done on natural fibers.
- *Dry Blocking:* This is similar to steam blocking; however, in the dry blocking method, you use no form of moisture and simply pin your fabric to a blocking mat and iron it.

Materials Used for Blocking:

- *T pins:* The pins used for blocking are shaped like a T with the pin side sharp to help pin the crochet fabric in place in spray and wet blocking methods. It is best to look for rust-proof t-pins and keep plenty of them because, like hair pins, these will vanish before you know it!
- *Wool Wash Detergent:* Just as the name suggests, detergents used for blocking are very mild, so it is important to choose the ones that are made for the blocking process. You can get the bar form or the liquid form; it is up to your preference.
- *Spray Bottle:* For liquid detergents, it is important to keep a separate empty spray bottle to help evenly spray the detergent on your crochet fabric. Look for heatproof ones, as you will be using warm water to spray on your fabric.
- *Blocking Mats:* These are usually made of rubber or foam that is used to pin down the crochet fabric for blocking. It helps ensure the fabric is pinned on an even and consistent surface. The material helps soak up the extra moisture from your fabric, making the drying part easier and faster.

How to Block Your Finished Project:

- Fill warm water into a clean basin and add your wool washing detergent (liquid or bar). Make sure the detergent is dissolved completely.
- Add in your crochet fabric by slowly pushing it into the warm detergent water to squeeze out any air bubbles.
- Let the project sit in the water for up to half an hour.
- Slowly pick the fabric from the water, making sure to support all of its weight with your hands so it does not stretch out. And gently squeeze out all of the excess water.
- Place it on a towel and roll it up to gently remove more moisture.
- Now place the fabric flat on a blocking mat and adjust the size and shape according to your desire.
- Now pin the garment to the block to help retain its shape.
- Lastly, let the fabric air dry completely on its own. This might take about 24 hours.

Chapter 2:
Your Crochet How-Tos

Before starting crocheting, there are different terms and techniques you might want to master. Like any other craft, crocheting is all about holding the tools the right way and learning the basic terms and stitches to help you get started on your journey.

How to Hold Your Yarn and Hook?

After the crochet hook, your yarn is the second essential tool necessary for all your crochet projects. I mean, how can you crochet if you do not have any kind of thread or yarn, right? In the last chapter, you learned about the different kinds of yarn you can use and what ways you can choose the perfect yarn for your project. Before you understand how to hold your yarn, it is important to learn about another important factor of thread/string-based craft: tension.

Tension

Tension is the amount of stress you apply to your yarn while using it. It means the way we pull our yarn from the skein while crocheting. A better way of understanding this is how Goldilocks from the tale The Goldilocks and the three bears once said, you do not want your tension to be too tight and you do not want it too loose either, you want it to be just right! The tension of yarn can greatly affect the outcome of your project which is why it is so important to learn about holding the right tension while crocheting.

Different Ways to Hold Your Yarn

Now, let us take a look at the different ways you can hold your yarn in crochet.

The first way you can hold your yarn is to start unwinding your yarn and wrap it around your little finger of the left hand, then bring it under the two middle fingers and over the index finger. This way is perfect for tight crocheters that have trouble making loose stitches. The tension of the yarn is divided between the fingers, which makes it easier to have more uniform stitches. This is the perfect way to hold the yarn for those who are tighter crocheters.

The second way you can hold your yarn while crocheting is to loop it on your little finger and then hold it between your index and middle finger. The yarn should go over the ring finger, the middle finger, and the index finger as if you are weaving the yarn between your fingers. This way is perfect for tightening the tension of your yarn and making your stitches tighter.

Whatever method you use to hold your yarn comes down to your own comfort and personal preference. Just make sure the tension is in your yarn, not in your head!

Crocheting Difference between Right-Handed and Left-Handed

The majority of people in this world are right-handed, which is why most crafts and tutorials online focus on the right-handed way of instructions. However, what about left-handed people? How can they understand the tutorial instructions if they do not even hold the tools the way the instructor told them to? It is easy; you just mirror the exact instructions. In crochet, a right-handed crocheter will work from right to left in rows and go around anticlockwise. While a left-handed crocheter will work from the left to right side of a row and make rounds clockwise. The main point is to work in the opposite direction of what is explained. For left-handed crochet, the project would be a mirror image of that made by a right-handed crocheter. For instance, a simple row of double crochet made by a left-handed will be a mirrored version of that made by a right-handed. Although it is very important to closely examine the process to ensure there are no differences in the stitching process.

Know the Right and Wrong Side of Your Fabric

We all have been through the confusion of forgetting the right side of our crochet fabric, right? In the beginning, it can be hard to determine which is the right or wrong side of your crochet project. You have been flipping the fabric a thousand times but still cannot figure out which is the right side and which is the wrong side. Let me help release you from your misery by telling you some tips and tricks that will come in handy when you get stuck on the wrong side of this craft. Before jumping onto the tips, let me first explain what exactly the right side and the wrong side of any crochet fabric are:

- Right side (RS): This is the side that is intended to face the outwards side of the project. This is often the neat side of the project that gives your project a neat and finished look.

- Wrong Side (WS): This is the side that is not visible once the project is finished like in bags or sweaters. This side of the fabric helps you hide any knots or color changes in your project.

While two of these sides are logical, some crochet stitches happen to produce a reversible fabric which can make it tricky for you to identify the back or front of your project. In such cases, it is important to determine the side which you want to be the front side and stick with it so it does not have any bumps, knots, or color changes.

How Do You Tell the Right Side Of A Crochet Project?

Now, let's talk about some easy tricks that will help you differentiate between the right and wrong sides of your crochet fabric or project.
- *Chain Tail Position:* An easy way of determining the right or wrong side of your work is by using the tail end of your foundation chain as a reference. Put your fabric flat in front of you and look at your work, the yarn tail will be at the bottom left of your fabric if you are right-handed. This means that you are looking at the right side of your fabric. If the tail is on the bottom right, you are looking at the wrong side of your work. For left-handed crocheters, this will be the opposite. The yarn tail should be on the bottom right to determine the right side of your work.
- *Count The Rows:* The starting row of your project will be the right side. This does not include the foundation chain, so the first row of single or double crochet stitches will determine your right-sided fabric. If you are using a pattern design that says otherwise the right side should always be a row with odd numbers. You can also use stitch markers to help you mark the right side of your fabric.
- *Using Round as Reference:* When you are working in rounds it is much easier to tell the right side of your crochet fabric or project. Projects like crochet granny squares are not

instructed to turn your work as the right side will always be facing you. The side with stitches that are more uniform and less bumpy is your right side.

- *The Best Side is The Right Side:* This trick is a safety net that has saved many crocheters. If you already have not determined the right side for your crochet project, the best advice I can give you is to pick the best-looking side!

Yarn Beginning End and Middle

One of the essential tools after a crochet hook is the yarn you use for crochet, without a good understanding of how to go about your yarn you will not be able to crochet the right way. Just as we have discussed in the previous chapter before using any hank of yarn you need to unwind it into a ball and then use it for crocheting. In the following, you will learn ways to join a new yarn in your current project and how to weave the ends or tails of your yarn.

How to Join a New Yarn

It is almost impossible to finish a project with a ball of yarn, especially if you are a lover of long and big crochet projects like I am. Joining a new yarn when you are halfway through your project can be tricky, so I will tell you multiple ways you can attach a new yarn to your project.

Note: These are not valid for when you want to change the colors of your yarn besides the first one!

Stitch the New Yarn with the Last Yarn

The easiest and fastest way to join crochet yarn into the fabric is by grabbing the new yarn and continuing crocheting seamlessly. Joining your new yarn ball with the last one over a crochet stitch is especially good if you want to change the colors of your yarn, just as you do in tapestry crochet. However, it is not one of the most secure methods, as the stitches can come apart pretty easily, so you have to make sure to weave the ends in. Here is how you will do it in an easy way:

Crochet your fabric until only 5 inches are left in your working yarn. Now, start a new stitch but do not complete it. You will draw up the stitch but stop before doing the final yarn over. For example, if you are doing a single crochet, you insert the hook into the stitch then yarn over and STOP! Now you will grab your new yarn and complete the stitch with it. In simpler words, continue the yarn over with your new yarn and pull through the remaining loops on your crochet hook. And simply continue to crochet with your new yarn. Make sure to gently tug the two yarn ends a couple of times after you have crocheted a few stitches with the new yarn. This will help secure the yarns together, so it does not come off while you are crocheting. After you finish your project make sure you weave those ends properly to avoid any unwinding of the stitches.

Note: This is also helpful while doing Tapestry Crochet.

Using the Magic Knot

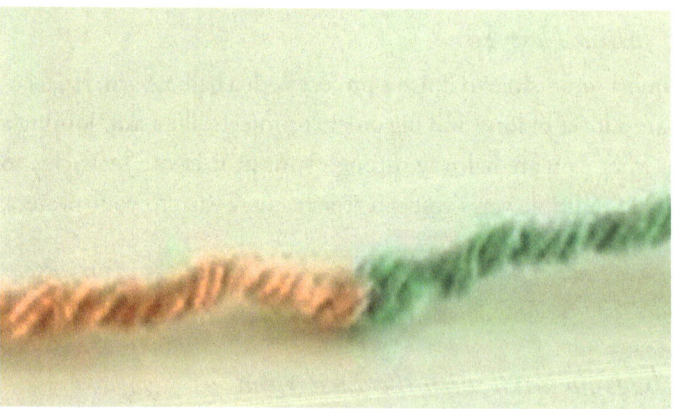

As the name states, this is a special technique that you can easily use in any crochet project. I use it all of the time in my projects. It is a tiny, barely noticeable, and surprisingly strong knot. You will find a lot of different ways to make a magic knot online; however, the one I am about to explain is the easiest and makes the most sense to me! You can tie it using any yarn type or fiber. Here is how you tie this magic knot:

Stop crocheting till you have about 10-12 inches of working yarn left. For starters it is always better to have more yarn to work with for better practice, as you get used to it you will only need half of it to tie the knot. Start by laying both working and new yarn parallel with the working yarn below and coming from the left and the new yarn coming from the right place above the working yarn. Now take the working yarn and it under then bring back over the new yarn and across itself. This will help you make a loop with the working yarn. Then, tie a knot with a working yarn pulling it tightly. Now, make a loop with the new yarn the same way you did with the working yarn, tie a knot, and pull it tight. Take both the working and the new yarn in each hand and pull them apart so the knots will slide together, pull tightly to secure the knot. Lastly, carefully trim the ends without cutting the knot or the joined yarn and you are done!

Note: This method is not for changing yarn colors!

Use the Russian Join

This technique is useful for joining new and working yarn with no ends to weave in. It can appear a little bit thicker; however, it is not noticeable once crocheted in. Here is how you can use it to join your yarn together:
- Start by threading your working yarn onto a needle. Make sure to thread it through the center of the working yarn for several inches.

- Pull the needle and yarn through gently, there should be a loop at the end.
- Thread the new yarn onto the same needle and then again thread it through the loop in the working yarn.
- Again, thread the new yarn through its own for several inches and pull the needle and yarn gently to form a loop.
- Lastly, smooth out the join by tugging on the yarn ends and carefully time the loose ends.

Using a Felted Join

Also known as the spit splice. The reason is that most people use their saliva to join in; however, I prefer using water, so that is what I will use in the explanation below. This method is used for joining yarns made from animal fibers as they have bards that can turn into felt with the help of moisture and friction. Here is how you can do it:
- Take some warm water and your yarn.
- Start unraveling the ends of both your yarns for about a couple of inches.
- Put the unraveled ends of the yarn in water for a couple of seconds.

- Shake off the excess moisture from the ends and place them in the palm of your hand in a way that they overlap each other.
- Now start rubbing your hands together so it causes friction that will help feel the ends together.
- Pause and check the strength of the join and see if no ends are sticking out. Rub again if necessary.

Note: You can try trimming the plies of each yarn end to help you give a nicer look to the joint. This is essential if you are working with yarn that has 4 or more plies. Trim out 2 plies from each end, then join as mentioned above!

How to Weave the Ends of Your Yarn Tails

An important finishing step to any crochet project is the weaving of yarn tails. This helps protect your project from unraveling when you wash or wear it. There are many different ways to weave in your yarn. However, I will tell you the easiest and simplest technique to help give your projects a secure, polished, and professional look!

Weaving in the ends or tails is a technique used to secure the loose ends of yarn at the end of your project. This prevents the yarn from unraveling and ensures that it looks neat and professional. It might sound like a tedious task however, it is an essential part of any crochet project.

Supplies Used to Weave Ends

All you need to weave in the ends professionally is a finished project and some tapestry needles. You have already read about tapestry needles and why they are used in your crochet projects. Make sure you have some good quality needles that are either made of plastic or steel as you deem fit for your project. The size should be thin and large enough so the yarn can be pulled through the eye of the needle easily.

How To Weave It

- Start by cutting off the yarn, leaving a long tail of almost 6 inches to weave in after finishing off the stitch of your project.

- Take a tapestry needle and thread the yarn tail through it.
- Now start weaving the ends horizontally or vertically through the base of the stitches.
- Work your way through one direction, then change directions again and weave it back through a few more stitches.
- Once you are done, pull the yarn snugly and then cut the yarn tail closest to the surface of the fabric.
- Lastly, stretch out the fabric so the end will get hidden between the stitches.

Note: Before you start weaving the ends, consider the type of project you will be weaving them into. Weave the ends on the wrong side of the work if possible. However, if you are working on a project with both sides, make sure to do your best to hide the ends as much as possible.

Know Your Basic Crochet Stitches

Every crochet beginner needs to learn the basic stitches and techniques that can help them create a variety of projects easily. Just like any craft crocheting stitches have little variations that can make your project a lot more beautiful, choosing the right stitch for your pattern is essential for getting the desired outcome for your project. So, let's learn some basic crocheting!

Yarn Over Vs. Yarn Under

Every stitch in crochet includes a "yarn over" in the instruction. But what does it mean to yarn over and how is it different from yarn under? These both are opposites and each one can make a huge difference in your crochet project. Let's learn about what these are and how you can yarn over and yarn under in crochet.

How to do Yarn Over?

- First start with the hook in front of the working yarn. Hold the hook in your dominant hand and control the yarn using the non-dominant hand.
- Press the hook and bring the yarn over the hook from back to front at the same time. The yarn should cross the front of the hook from upper right to lower left and vice versa if you are left-handed.

How to do Yarn Under?

- Start by doing the same as you did in the yarn over; however, bring the hook over the top of the working yarn so it crosses the front of your hook from the lower right to the upper left and vice versa for left-handers.

Slip Knot

The first step in almost any crochet project starts with making a slip knot. You can create it using multiple ways. One of the simplest methods of creating a slip or sliding knot is what you will learn here. Make sure you have a simple practicing yarn that is not too fuzzy or bright and a respective hook to go with your yarn. Once you have all your tools and supplies, let's get crocheting:

- *Hold your Yarn and Hook:* After choosing your material, hold your hook in one hand and the yarn in the other; make sure you are using your dominant hand for holding the hook and your non-dominant hand for holding the yarn. Leave about 4 inches of your yarn strand and choose your favorite way to hold the yarn, as we have discussed above. Either in a straight way or weaved way, whatever you are comfortable with. Use either pencil or knife grip to grasp your hook and relax your fingers so they have room to move freely; however, grip the hook tight enough to maintain precision.
- *Loop the Yarn on the Hook:* Hold the strand of yarn in your left hand while lifting your crochet hook slightly above your left and drape the yarn on the hook with the index finger of your right hand. Now, rotate the hook clockwise under the right and back to the starting position. In other words, you are turning the hook in a circle to make a loose loop on the hook.
- *Yarn Over your Hook:* Adjust your hand and pinch the tail of the yarn in between your middle finger and thumb while inserting your index finger between the yarn strand and up to the back to help unwind the yarn ball easily. Make a yarn over by wrapping the yarn over the hook from behind and then over the top.
- *Pull the Yarn through the loop:* Using the head of the crochet hook, pull the yarn over and through the loop on the hook. The yarn should overpass through the hoop and form a knot on the hook.
- *Tighten the loop knot:* Now you have a loose slip knot on your hook. So leave it on the hook and slightly pull both ends to tighten it just enough so it is snug but not excessively tight on the hook.

Slip Stitch

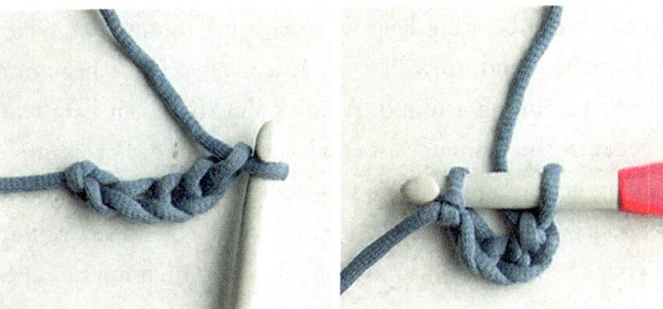

After the slip knot, a slip stitch is one of the basic crochets stitches every crocheter knows. You use a slip stitch to join pieces together, add decorative items to your project and finish projects with simple edging on the ends. There are many patterns where you will use a slip stitch as a way to work a smaller stitch as it is shorter than a single crochet; however, due to its high functionality, you can use it in lots of different ways. Now, let's move on to learning how to work a slip stitch!

- Start by inserting your hook and do a yarn over. You can make a slip stitch at any point in your project.
- If you have an active loop, simply insert your hook into the spot where you want to crochet the stitch and pull the yarn through the project.
- Finally, pull the new loop through the active loop on your hook and do this step a few times till it becomes a single motion.

Chapter 2: Your Crochet How-Tos | 45

Joining a Round with Slip Stitch

A slip stitch can be a big help when creating rounds in crochet. You can sometimes end up with a big space between the beginning and end when finishing a round. A quick slip stitch can help close the gap between the first and last stitch in the round. For example, when making granny squares, this technique is very common. Some patterns specify whether you will need to do this or not. If you are working your round in a continuous spiral, a slip stitch might not be necessary at all.

Single Crochet

Single crochet, as the name states, is a single looped stitch that is slightly different from a slip stitch. It is the shortest stitch, so you can use it in between different stitches to give you a variation in your pattern. Here is how you can work with this stitch:

Start by forming a stitches chain as a foundation row, then start inserting the hook into the first chain, leaving the first row and starting from the row in the second number and beyond; insert your crochet hook into the stitch directly under it. After that, slide your crochet hook under the loops on the upper part of the chain. After putting the crochet hook in the yarn, prepare to pull up a loop while wrapping the yarn over your crochet hook, then grab it with your crochet hook. Now start drawing your yarn and hook through the created loop. This will give you two working loops on your crochet hook. Again, wrap the yarn on your crochet hook making a loop, and then hook the yarn. Then, draw your yarn into the two loops you created, and you are done with your single crochet stitch!

Half-Double Crochet

After a single crochet stitch, this is the next basic crochet stitch you will need to learn. It is a beautifully versatile yet simple crochet stitch. It is taller than a single crochet stitch. It consists of three loops. Let's learn how to make this simple yet beautiful stitch!

After a slip knot, start making a foundation chain to work the first row into. It can be of any length; however, if you are following a specific pattern, it is better to follow the length instructed in it. Work into the chain that is three chains away from your hook. When crocheting in rows, use a turning chain. The height of the chain depends on the height of the crochet stitch. Do a yarn over and insert your crochet hook into your stitch. Yarn over again and pull the yarn through the stitch. This should give you three loops on your hook to work with. Lastly, do a yarn over one more time and pull the yarn through all three loops. The remaining loop is your connecting loop for the next stitch.

Double Crochet

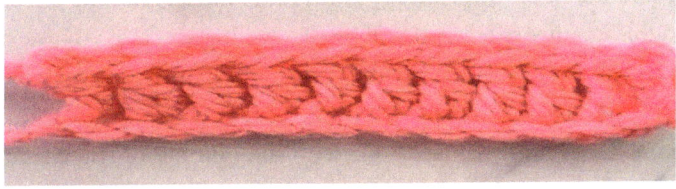

Every crochet journey begins with learning some basic crochet stitches. The double crochet is just like a half-double; however, it is a bit longer in length. Throughout your crochet journey, you will be using this stitch in many different ways.

- Like all the other basic stitches, start with a foundation chain. Start with a slip knot, then work on your crochet chain. If you are wormakeith a crochet pattern, make sure to read the length described in the instructions. For example, if you want to crochet a skinny scarf, that is 10 double crochet stitches across. Then make a foundation chain of 10 + 2 or 12 stitches. The extra twos are for the first double crochet.
- Do a yarn over your crochet hook, then insert the hook onto the chain. For the first stitch, you will insert the hook into the third chain from your hook. The chains that you are skipping are counted as your first double crochet of the row. However, you will not be able to see it until you finish the next stitch. These helped in creating the chains that became the first double crochet.
- Then, do a yarn over again and pull the yarn through the third chain from the hook; after finishing this step, you will have three loops on your crochet hook.
- Doing a yarn over once again, pull the yarn through the first two of the three loops on your hook. This leaves you back to 2 loops on your hook.
- Lastly, do a yarn over one last time and pull the yarn through both loops that are on the hook. And you are done with your first double crochet stitch!

After you are done with this, you will find yourself looking at another double crochet stitch that will be the starting stitch of your next stitch. You will only need to skip the first three chains at the very beginning of the row. After that, you do not need to skip; just continue the same steps until you are done with the number of stitches required for your pattern!

How to Double Crochet Two Stitches Together

Double crocheting two stitches together is a special technique that you can use in many different projects. Let's learn how it is done!

- Start by doing a yarn over by inserting the hook into the next stitch and pulling up a loop so you are left with three loops on the hook.
- Yarn over again and pull through just the first two loops, and now you have again two loops remaining on your hook.
- Do another yarn over and insert the hook into the next stitch, then pull up a loop so you have four loops on the hook.
- Then, do another yarn over and pull through just the first two loops again, with three loops remaining on your crochet hook.
- Lastly, do a last yarn over and pull through all the remaining three loops.

Now you have completed a double two-stitch together! Continue in the next stitch for the number of stitches needed before moving on to the next row.

Treble Crochet

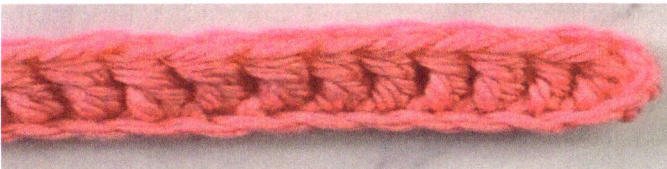

A treble crochet stitch is a tad bit longer than your regular double crochet stitch. It is often used to make dense fabric. Let's start on how to practice a treble crochet stitch using a simple practicing yarn and matching crochet hook!

- Start by doing a yarn over the hook twice, then insert the hook into the next stitch.
- Do another yarn over the hook and pull the yarn through the stitch so you have four loops on your crochet hook.
- Loop your yarn over your hook again and draw through two loops only. So now you have three working loops on your crochet hook.

Chapter 2: Your Crochet How-Tos | **49**

- Yarn over your hook again and draw through just the first two loops.
- Lastly, do another loop yarn over your crochet hook and draw through the last two loops on the hook so you are left with one working loop to help you start the next stitch.

Now your treble crochet stitch is done. You will learn about how to make a turning chain and create rows of treble crochet stitches in the upcoming heading, so keep reading on!

Chain Stitch

After learning to make a slip knot, the next step in your crocheting journey is to learn how to make a series of chain stitches. These are the foundations of your project. A project is always built on chain stitches. This is why it is one of the essential stitches that every beginner needs to learn before starting to crochet. There are many ways you can use a chain stitch in your project; apart from being the foundation of your crochet project, chain stitches are often scattered throughout the rest of the design. They are usually combined with other stitches to form patterns and create spaces between motifs and shapes. You can even use a simple chain on its own to use as laces for baby booties, a decorative string for typing gifts, and hanging ornaments. Let's learn how to make a basic chain stitch:

- Start by making a slip knot on your hook and grasp the knot between the thumb and middle finger of your non-dominant hand. With the slip stitch facing you, weave the yarn between your fingers to help create equal tension in your stitches. Make sure to keep a tight and controlling grip on the hook, as you will need to rotate it as you make the chain stitches.

- Now loop your yarn over the hook from back to front as you would do a yarn over.
- Pull the yarn through the loop by rotating your crochet hook by one-quarter turn, then pull the hood down and through the current loop on the hook. Do not forget to bring the hook back to its original upwards position.
- Now once you have made the first chain stitch it is easier to continue as you can draw a loop and pull through, repeating this motion as many times as necessary. As you work through it, you will eventually find a rhythm that will help you maintain uniform tension in your stitches.

Foundation Chain

Also known as the base or starting chain, the first series of chain stitches at the beginning of a project right after a slip knot is called the foundation chain. After that, you can easily work the first row of stitches into your chain to start making your crochet fabric.

Counting Chain

The next step after learning how to do a foundation chain is to learn how to count your chain or stitches. Every crochet pattern starts with a definite number of chains you need; even with a swatch of fabric, you need to carefully count the stitches before continuing. This is where row counters come in handy. It might look simple, but there are a few things you need to remember when counting your crochet stitches!

- It is very easy to count stitches if you look at them from above. Start by placing your fabric on a table and search for the 'v' shape; every 'v' counts as a stitch.
- You do not count a slip knot or loop on your hook as a stitch.
- Never work through the first chain from your crochet hook; always work into the second, third, and fourth so on a chain. The instruction of any pattern will tell you how many chains to skip before starting your first stitch.

Turning Chain

The length of any turning chain depends on the height of your crochet stitches. Tall stitches require more chain stitches, and short stitches require fewer chains. For example, if you are working with a single crochet stitch, you will use a single chain stitch as a turning chain. You will keep adding one more as you use half double, double, treble, and double treble crochet stitches. It usually takes the place of the first stitch of the row except for single crochet rows. When working on single crochet rows, you would work to the end of a row. Simply turn over your crochet fabric and make one chain stitch, then work the first stitch of the new row into your pattern. However, with double or other taller stitches, you would work to the end of the row. Start by turning over your crochet piece, then make a chain of the number of stitches required as the turning chain. You will count as the first stitch of the row and work the second stitch in your pattern.

Chain Stitch Rings

When you are crocheting a round shape, and one way is by starting by crocheting a number of chains in your pattern and then joining them into a circle. Here is how you can do it:

- To join your chain into a circle first, insert your crochet hook into the first chain after the slip knot and yarn around the hook.
- Then, pull the yarn through the chain and the loop on your hook at the same time. This will create a slip stitch and form a circle.

And voila! Now you have a chain ring to work into your pattern as instructed.

Chain Space

A small space you have under a chain the previous round or between other stitches is called a chain space. Filling this space is easy as the stitches are made directly into the chain space and not into the chain itself. After you are done making a chain, you will be instructed to make a number of chains to bring your fabric to the right height for the first stitch of the first round. Keeping an eye on where the center of the ring is very important, so you can try sticking your finger into the hold to help define it. You can always smooth this up later while sewing in the end. If you feel like you are running out of space in the ring, then you can try to ease up your stitches so they are more bunched up to give you more space on the right. However, be careful not to make your new stitches over the top of the first stitches or chains made in this round.

Increase and Decrease Stitches

Some patterns in crochet require an increase or decrease in your stitches. To do that, you simply add or join stitches together to reduce the stitch count. Here you will learn about how increases and decreases in stitches work out in any crochet pattern.

Increasing Stitches

In crochet, we typically put one stitch in each stitch from the previous row. However, when it comes to increasing the stitch count, you simply place 2 or more stitches in the stitch from the previous row. An increase can be made anywhere from the previous row's beginning, end, or middle. You can make your fabric wider by placing the increases at the beginning or end of the row. And placing increases in the middle of the row can cause the fabric to blow up or out at the place with the increases. You can use the same technique for any kind of stitch; just place 2 of the same stitch into the stitch on the row below.

Decreasing Stitches

When decreasing, you typically work two stitches together. Unlike the increasing technique, the decreasing stitches have different techniques for each of the basic stitches. Let's see how you can decrease different kinds of stitches.

- Single Crochet Decrease: First, identify the stitches you want to decrease; you can use stitch markers to mark them if you want. Using your crochet hook, pull up a loop in the first of the 2 stitches. So, you will have 2 loops on the hook. And then again, pull a loop in the second of the 2 stitches. Now, you have 3 loops left on your crochet hook. Lastly, yarn over and pull through all 3 loops on the hook, and you are done!
- Half Double Crochet Decrease: Same as the above technique, you will first identify the 2 stitches you need to decrease. Then, you will yarn over and pull the loop on both stitches one by one. Now, you will have 5 working loops left on your crochet hook. Lastly, yarn over and pull through all 5 loops on the hook.
- Double Crochet Decrease: This is a little different than the other technique. After identifying the 2 stitches you want to decrease, take your hook and yarn over and pull a loop in the first of the 2 stitches so you will have 3 loops on your hook. Then, yarn over and pull through 2 loops on the hook so you are left with 2 loops on your hook. Do the same thing with your second stitch, then yarn over and pull through all 3 loops on your hook.

Front Vs. Back Loops

Every stitch on a crochet fabric has a small 'v' shape at the top, that is made up of two loops, a front loop, and a back loop. People often get confused between the two due to their similarities. A good way to identify this is by checking the distance. The closest one to you is the front loop, and the one further away from you is the back loop. This means that it can change depending on which side of the stitch you are looking at. The front and back loops will look different whether you are working in rounds and not turning your work compared to when you are turning rounds and working in rows.

Mostly, you would insert your crochet hook under both the loops that make up the top 'v' shape. However, sometimes the instructions of a certain pattern will tell you to work into only the front or back loop. You can do that by inserting your crochet hook under only the specified loop instead of all the loops altogether. This causes a change in the angle of the stitch which can create a ribbed fabric. This technique also turns your work in different directions when working on three-dimensional objects. For instance, when you are working on a post topper, scraper mitt, or sweater vest. The choice of which loop you want to work on depends on the kind of effect you are looking for. Working with only the front loop gives you an exposed loop on the back and vice versa for the back loop. When working in the front loops, your project fabric will tilt forward, and working in the back loop will tilt your project fabric backward. So do try this technique if you want to give your work a unique texture!

Working in Rounds

For beginners, it is always advised to work on choosing patterns that are worked flat in rows, like scarves, baby blankets, and washcloths. These are wonderful as your startup projects; however, you do not need to limit yourself to these. Crocheting rounds can help you achieve a broader range of projects, such as hats, mittens, and booties, to just name a few. The possibilities are limitless once you are more comfortable with the technique. Working in rounds can be hard for beginners; however, with the right guidance and tools, you are set up for a good start!

To start with, grab a smooth worsted weight yarn in a bright color for practicing along with a crochet of 5.5 mm and follow along with the instructions given below!

- The first step is to create your beginning loop, which will be the center of your ring or round. You will be creating your first round of stitches into this ring center. So, start by chaining 4 stitches and work a slip stitch into the first chain. This will help create a foundation to build your stitches. And this will be referred to as the center ring.
- Next, you will create your first round of stitches. For your practice Swatch, start by making single crochet stitches. Start by inserting your hook through the center of the ring, not onto the individual stitch, then yarn over and pull through 2 loops on your yarn. Do that throughout the center ring so you will have a total of 7 single crochet stitches.
- Then, after you are done with the seven single crochet stitches through your center ring, make a slip stitch into the chain 1 you made at the beginning of the round. This stitch will join your first and last stitches together and finish your round. Then you will continue to make stitches by counting the first chain of every round as one single crochet stitch, which means your completed round consists of 8 stitches altogether. You can increase or decrease the number of stitches required according to your project; however, the foundation technique will be the same.
- Lastly, to continue your rounds, a good rule is to increase every stitch in round 2, every other stitch in round 2, every third stitch in round 4, and so on. For instance, for increase round 1, you will have chain 1, working 2 single crochets in every stitch around, a slip stitch to join, so a total of 16 stitches in the entire round. The number of stitches will double after

adding 1 stitch for every original stitch. You will continue the same with the rest of your rounds. In the second round, you will have chain 1, then 1 single crochet stitch in the next stitch, 2 single crochet in the next stitch, and do this 8 times, then make a slip stitch to join so you end up with a total of 24 stitches. You will do the same for the following rounds.

Magic Circle

A magic circle in crochet is like an adjustable ring that is a very useful technique for crocheting in the round. It can help eliminate pesky holes that can form in the center of your work. To make an adjustable circle, you will first make a round of stitches and turn it into an adjustable loop. Then, you can simply pull the yarn tail to close the loop tightly. Like any other crocheting technique, this one also had many different ways to demonstrate it. I will teach you the simplest and easiest way of making a magic circle. It has two working parts, the first is the adjustable loop, and the second is the main pattern stitches. Now, let's get crocheting!

- Start by placing your yarn ball on the table and lay down the tail end of your yarn on your open non-dominant hand.

Then loop the end of the yarn near the ball around your first two fingers, so they make a parallel line of two strands at the back of your hand. Now, pinch the intersecting part of the yarn between your thumb and index finger.

- Use your crochet hook and slide it under the right-hand piece of yarn and over the left-hand piece of yarn. Pull a loop using the yarn on your left-handed side.
- Holding the loop in your left hand. Start wrapping the working yarn from back to front over the hook and pull the yarn through the loop on your hand to make a chain. However, this one does not count as a stitch. The number of chain stitches will depend on the type of stitch you used for the first round. So, for a single crochet, you will only make a chain; for a half double crochet you will make 2 chains, and so on.
- Insert your hook into the center of the ring and yarn over a loop to begin your first single crochet. Make sure you crochet over both the loop and the yarn tail. Do a yarn over and pull the yarn through both strands. And continue making stitches until you have the required number you need for your pattern.
- Now, hold your stitches with the fingers of your right hand. And use your left hand to pull the yarn tail to adjust the circle like a drawstring bag.
- Once you reach the desired tightness of the circle, you will work a slip stitch into the first stitch to join the round and continue with the pattern.

How to Embroider in Crochet

A great way to embellish your crochet fabric is through embroidery. You can create color and texture in your crochet fabric simply by adding a few stitches at the end of your project. Embroidery can help you add interesting patterns on a plain background or details on your projects. Embroidery helps you customize your projects in your unique way. The basic supplies you will need are some tapestry needles, a crochet hook, and embroidery thread or yarn. Now, let's jump to how to embroider some of the basic embroidery stitches.

The first step to any crochet embroidery stitch is to start by inserting the thread or yarn through the needle eye and securing it at the backside of your crochet fabric, where you wish to start the embroidery pattern. To avoid knots, try weaving the thread into the back of the fabric stitches and then start your embroidery.

- Cross Stitch Embroidery: After doing the initial step, bring your needle from the back to the front of the fabric, where you wish to start your cross stitch. Push down the needle into the top right corner of the square you want to form a diagonal line. Then, bring the needle up in the bottom right corner then insert it again into the top left corner of the square. Pull the thread to make a cross and repeat the first step.
- Backstitch Embroidery: Start by bringing your needle from the back to the front of the fabric, doing one hole to the right of the desired start of your backstitch line. Then push the needle through the fabric one stitch to the left. Bring the needle back to the front two stitches to the right, then again push the needle back one stitch to the left. This will join the line, then repeat step 2, moving horizontally, diagonally, or vertically to create a length of your desired length.
- French Knot Embroidery: Bring the needle from the back to the front where you wish to place your knot. Then using your thumb and forefinger, hold the thread after it comes from the fabric and twist the needle thrice. Push the needle back in the fabric as close to the start as possible. Holding the thread tight, push the twists of thread to sit up next to the fabric and push the needle gently through the knot to secure it on the surface of the fabric.

Now you have learned all the basic stitches and techniques used in crochet! Keep on reading to master this yarnful craft!

Chapter 3: Variations and Finishing

Variations in Stitches

After you have mastered the basic stitches in crochet, you can combine them to make different variations to create different kinds of fabric. Some advanced crochet stitches can be built using the foundations' crochet stitches, such as half double, double, treble, and other longer crochet stitches. Combining these different stitches can result in a terrific texture of the fabric. It might seem overwhelming at first; however, minor variations can be made from the foundation of basic stitches in crochet. Let's jump on how these variations can be made!

Shell Stitch

Starting from one of the basic stitch variations in crochet. This stitch requires no joining; all you have to do is crochet the number of stitches in the same stitch. The most common will be crocheting a five dc or double-crochet shell stitch. Do your double crochet stitch into the desired stitch where you want your shell stitch, then make 4 more of the same stitch into the current working stitch, and that's it. You have made a 5 double crochet shell stitch. Normally, you can skip spaces after and before placing your shell stitch. You can use any basic crochet

stitch and number of basic stitches. For instance, work an 8-half double crochet into the same stitch. For a more advanced version of shell stitch, you can use different height stitches into the same shell, for instance, 2 single crochet, 2 half double crochet, 1 single crochet, and 2 double crochet works into a single stitch. It can also include chain stitches. This is a versatile stitch, so you can create variations as you like.

Clusters Stitch

The cluster crochet stitch variation is like a bobble stitch in which you will start by crocheting stitches one after another in a series and leave the last loop of each stitch unfinished until you are done and then secure all the unfinished loops to create a single stitch. However, unlike bobble stitches, you will work on individual stitches subsequently in the cluster stitch variation. So learning where and how to insert your crochet hook for each "leg" of the cluster will help you master this variation in no time!

Let's work on a 5 double crochet or dc cluster stitch variation. Start by doing a dc into the stitch where you want to start your cluster variation stitch and leave the final loop on your hook. Do a yarn over, then insert hook into stitch, yarn over again and pull through, yarn over again and pull through 2 loops. Skip the final yarn over the step you would normally do in a double crochet and repeat the sequence into each of the next stitches, then yarn over, pulling through all 5 stitches.

Cluster stitch variations are often used for decreasing techniques. Your 2 double crochet is the same as decreasing double crochet or doing a double crochet 2 together you have learned in the previous chapter. These stitch variations are often used in decreasing techniques and can be worked in all your basic stitches. Just like any stitch variation, you can join a different combination of stitches into a cluster just by leaving the last loop unfinished of each stitch on the hook until you are done, then join them together.

Bobbles Stitch

Another variation of your basic stitch is called a bobble stitch, where you will combine multiple unfinished stitches into the same loop and secure them at the top of your fabric to make small bubbles

Chapter 3: Variations and Finishing | **63**

of stitches. This is a lot like the popcorn stitch variation, but you will not remove any stitch from your crochet hook until the very end of your stitch.

Let's demonstrate by working on a 5 double crochet bobbles stitch variation. Start your double crochet stitch where you want your variation bobbles, then leave the final loop on your hook. So do your yarn over, insert your crochet hook, then yarn over, pulling through, then do this again with 2 loops but skip the last step. Do the same step four more times so you have five unfinished double crochet stitches worked into the same stitch and six loops on your crochet hook. Close your stitch will the yarn over and draw through all loops on the hook. Now you have finished your five double crochet bobbles stitch variations!

You can work with the bobbles variations using any basic crochet stitch and with any number of stitches to create a variety in your pattern.

Popcorns Stitches

After you master the crochet shell variation stitch, you can easily make popcorn variation stitch. The initial process is the same as you crochet all stitches into the same stitch. However, in a popcorn stitch, the joining will be done at the top. So if you are doing a five-double crochet stitch. Do the same thing as you would in a normal shell stitch;

start with a double crochet where you want to place your variation popcorn stitch, then make 4 more stitches of the same kind so you have a 5 double crochet shell variation stitch. Now what you will do is remove the hook from the last stitch, then reinsert it from front to back into the top of the first stitch in the group. Lastly, pick up the working loop of the 5th stitch and pull it through the top of the 1st stitch to close it up. You can use this stitch variation for all of the basic crochet stitches!

Puff Stitch

The puff variation stitch is the same as the bobble variation stitch. However, you only use a half-double crochet stitch for this variation, unlike the bobble stitch which is used by working with longer stitches. The uniqueness of the third loop in your basic half double crochet stitch makes this puff variation stitch different from regular bobble stitch. Start by doing a yarn over and inserting your crochet hook where you want to start your puff variation stitch, then yarn over and pull through. Do this four times so you have 11 working loops on your hook for a puff variation of 5 half double crochet stitches. Lastly, pull through all the created loops on your crochet hook after doing the last yarn over, and you are done!

Note: You will need to work an extra chain stitch to secure your puff stitch firmly into your crochet fabric!

Basket Weave Stitch

You can make a beautiful crochet fabric with amazing texture using a basket weave variation stitch. It is perfect for making a thick, dense, warm, and cozy fabric without any holes in between to make baby blankets and so on. The main variation stitch is used by both back and front post stitches. You will mostly see tutorials using a double crochet post stitch for making basket weave fabric; however, you can easily do it with any of the other taller stitches of your choice. The main key is to weave a stitch of the same number for front and back post stitches; for instance, first, you will do five front post stitches, then follow it by doing five back post stitches, and so on. You can use any alternative number pattern of your choice to make it; however, make sure both the front and back post stitches are of the same numbered length.

Start with a chain with numbers equal to your stitch number choice plus added number for the turning chain, so for a double crochet stitch with five stitch rows, you will make a chain with eight stitches long. Then after laying your foundation chain, start by crocheting your chosen stitch with each stitch across. Start your post stitches with the turning chain and alternate between front post and back post stitches across the row in groups. Try ending the row with a chosen stitch in the top to give it an even edge. Then finish your desired number of rows for your first set, then reverse the direction so that instead of working a front-to-back post in the first set, you will do a back-to-front post in your next set of rows. Keep doing this till you have reached your desired blanket size, and add a border by weaving in the end. This will give your project a bit more structure!

V-Stitch

This variation is very quick to make and is a useful technique for working on different crocheting projects like Afghans. So let's learn how to make this beautiful and versatile stitch variation. Starting with a foundation chain of 10 stitches. Then crochet a double crochet stitch in the 4th chain, so you have two double crochet stitches to make a nice start. Then, skip the chain and work another double crochet stitch into the next chain. This will be your first half V stitch which will separate the stitch at the top. Now make another double crochet stitch into the same stitch you worked on to finish your first V stitch. For the next variation, stitch yarn over to begin your double crochet stitch, then skip two chains and crochet your first double crochet stitch, then your second one in the same stitch to complete your second v stitch. Repeat until you reach the end of your row, then work a chain stitch and a double crochet stitch into the last two stitches to make a matching edge at the beginning of the row. Now work another 3 chain stitches as your turning chain, then turn over to crochet the second row working across your first row. Count your turning chain as the first stitch, then work another double crochet into the next stitch. Now work every new V stitch into the middle of the stitch worked in the row below by placing your hook in the space between the V instead of the chain stitch. Then continue until your reach your desired length and weave in the ends!

Finishing Techniques

After working hours on your project, choosing the correct finishing technique can be crucial. You do not want to choose one that makes your project look different than what you imagined. There are many different edging techniques that you can use to weave in the ends of your project and give them a nice clean border. A simple change in the edge or border of your project can make it go from "okay" to "wow!" Learn these techniques to make your projects look even more unique and spectacular!

Shell Stitch Edge

The shell stitch can be a great way of adding a quick edge to your project. You can use it to add a single row at the bottom of any one side of your crochet fabric. It can be made using a double crochet stitch with chain spaces and slip stitches to separate each row. It is great for beginners who want to give uniqueness to their crochet projects, such as a side border for your cushion cover or a hem edging to your crochet sweater and so on.

Let's start on how to crochet a shell stitch edge to your project. If you are using the same yarn, then just finish your project as you like and turn the work around; then, crochet a slip knot into the first stitch of the row. However, if you are using a different yarn for edging, suppose a different colored yarn, then you finish the project along with weaving the ends in, then join your new yarn in the top right corner of your work with a slip knot of the edging yarn on the hook then the same thing you would do when you are using the same yarn. So make a slip stitch in the first stitch of the row you want to add your edge to. Leaving the next two stitches work, five double crochet stitches separated by a chain stitch, working them into the same space again leave two stitches, then make a slip stitch into the third stitch. Repeat this step until you complete your row until you reach the end, then secure with a slip stitch again. Make sure to weave in the edges if you wish to add the edging to only one row to help secure your work.

Picot Stitch Edge

This edging technique can be a little tricky for beginners; however, with practice, you will find it to be the most easily done finishing technique. All you have to do is make a few chains followed by a slip stitch at the end of the chain. You can easily adjust the number of chains to match the look and size of your project. This technique can be used to add decoration on the edge of a crochet piece, or you can even use them to give your project a lacy edge. You can make it in different sizes depending on your preference or the size of your project.

- Small: Start by making a foundation chain using a row of single crochet stitches. Then work 1 stitch into each of the first 2 stitches. Now make a slip stitch into the first chain and single crochet into each of the next 2 stitches, then repeat till you reach the end of your row.
- Medium: Do the same as you have done in the small picot edging; just crochet into 3 stitches instead of one, then repeat till you reach the end of your row.
- Large: To make your picot edging bigger, all you have to do is work into 4 stitches altogether to make it bigger and repeat what you did in the small picot edging. Keep repeating the same stitch technique till you reach the end of your row.

Note: *This edge can be done using any of the straight and firm stitches, such as the single crochet, double crochet, and trebles crochet stitches. You can easily use this when you want a neat, firm edge or between a net fabric to add a good and firm texture to it.*

Crab Stitch Edge

This stitch will give your work a firm and plain edge. You can easily work with it to give your project some neatness. It can be tricky to work with in the beginning because it is stitched backward, and the stitches will twist in a way that gives it some neatness. It is usually used for edging your fabric; however, you can use this stitch to make an entire piece of fabric too!

Let's see how you make this beautiful edge. Start by making a foundation with straight-edged stitches like you used for picot edging. You will work on this stitch backward, so you do not have to make a working chain or turn your work. So, just insert your crochet hook into the last stitch of your row, then make a single crochet stitch and simply repeat it working all along the row from left to right. It can look simple; however, working backward can be a real task for beginners, so make sure you get a lot of practice before using it for one of your big projects.

Blanket Stitch Edge

This stitch is your traditional edging technique used to close the edge of blankets since old times. You will find a lot of blanket patterns explaining the use of this stitched edge as it is used to secure the edging of blankets and comforters. It can be tricky for the first few stitches; however, it all comes down to getting used to the technique!

Before you start your edging, make sure you have a colored piece of yarn and some tapestry needles, then pass the yarn through the hole of the needle and secure the end with a knot. Hold your fabric and insert your needle from the back at the place you want to start your edge. Then poke your needle again down to the back, leaving a ¼ inch distance between where you inserted the needle and the edge of the fabric. Now again, bring your needle from back to front so you have a straight line right at the bottom of the edge piece. However, before tightening this stitch, make sure to needle through the loop you created while holding the thread so it starts under the needle. Now repeat this till you reach the end of the edging row.

If you run out of thread, you can easily start by poking your needle where you want to start the next stitch and pull the thread till you only have enough for a loop, then cut and knot off the tail end of the thread close to the fabric so the loose loop stays in place. Now thread your needle with the new yarn and knot the end like you did at first. Poke the needle from the back at the bottom of the edge and complete your stitch by sliding it under the loose loop you create, then pull your stitch to tighten it. Lastly, finish your edging by poking your needle at the right side down to the back of your last stitch and knot off your thread.

Single Crochet Join

Joining stitches are used to join multiple pieces of crochet fabric together to get your finished project. Different patterns and projects require you to work on small pieces of different crochet fabrics and then join them all together at the end to get your desired outcome. This is a simple joining technique to help you join a new crochet fabric in your project. Single crochet join is just like your typical single crochet; however, this time, you will be using this for edging and joining new yarn into your work. Start by placing a slip knot with your new yarn on your crochet hook and insert it into the stitch you want to continue with your new yarn. Do a yarn over and draw a loop through the stitch and so on as you would do for a single crochet stitch, then repeat till you reach the end of your row.

Slip Stitch Join

Another way to join; however, this time, you will do a slip stitch which is shorter than the single crochet stitch which you learned previously. So to start, you will insert your hook on the desired starting stitch, then use a slip knot to secure the yarn on your crochet hook, then draw the knot through the stitch and first chain of your fabric. Proceed with the pattern as you desire to work.

Backstitch Join

Another useful technique used for joining crochet pieces together is by sewing them using a backstitch. It involves placing your pieces with the right sides together and sewing in and out along the seam line with tapestry needles. Start by pinning your fabrics together, making sure the stitches align in the same place, and if you happen to have a longer or wider piece, you have to ease in the extra fabric to

help balance the pieces in place. Then, take thread your tapestry needle with your yarn and place the stitch between the strands of yarn instead of through them. Start with the binding stitch by going around the edge and coming back to the same spot to secure the end of the yarn, then bring the bottom edges of your pieces together. Now, go around again and come back out from the first stitch farther up from the initial stitch. The needle needs to go in and out along the running stitches between the first two stitches you have already created. Then, insert the needle back through the initial stitch again and bring the tip out through both layers again. Now, proceed with this manner going forward and coming back as you would do in a typical backstitch, keeping an even tension. Now you are done with learning all the different finishing techniques of crocheting. Congratulations! And keep on reading for more wonderful information about crochet.

Chapter 4:
Save Yourself from Making These Newbie Mistakes

Crochet is an art form that has been enjoyed for centuries, and it is no surprise that beginners often make mistakes when they first start. Crochet beginners may make a variety of mistakes, such as losing count of their stitches, accidentally increasing or decreasing the number of stitches in a row, not knowing where to start their stitches, how to keep count of rows, not learning about different time-saving techniques or not understanding the importance of choosing the right crochet hook and yarn. These mistakes can be frustrating, but they are also a natural part of the learning process. In this chapter, we will explore some of the most common mistakes made by crochet beginners and provide tips and tricks to help you avoid them. By reading this chapter, you will be able to save yourself from making these mistakes and make the most out of your crochet experience. With this knowledge, you can confidently begin your crochet journey and create beautiful projects that you will be proud of.

Stitch Your Hook in the Wrong Chain When Starting a Project

The first stitch that you learn in crochet is the chain stitch which is a foundational stitch that you use to build your project. Making a starting chain is the least enjoyable part of any project. One mistake that we make when crocheting is we do not know how to hook in the correct chain when starting a crochet project. The patterns always say to start crocheting in the second chain from the hook; however, all the loops look the same, so how do we know which chain is the correct one to start your project? After you are done crocheting the number of chain stitches asked in the pattern, you will have a strand made of chain stitches. The first chain is the loop currently on your crochet hook, and the second chain is the one after it. You can easily confuse it with the bottom part of the loop on your hook; however, you have to go to the second loop, which is the second chain. Now you will work down the row of chain stitches and work a stitch into the loops you created with the chain stitches till you get to the end. Another thing you can do is lay your project flat on a surface and straighten it so you can see where the stitches are and how to work up your next stitch.

Starting Loops with Linked Chain Instead of a Magic Loop

Crocheting in rounds can be done using two different ways. First is to start by making a chain of 4 or 5 stitches, then join it in a circle with a slip stitch. Another way that I often use is by using the magic circle technique you have learned in the previous chapter. Beginners are often taught to use the chain method when learning to crochet granny squares. However, using a magic circle creates a neater and tighter look compared to the chain ring method. Ultimately, both methods are correct, and the choice comes down to personal preference. However, if you do not want to end up with an awkward space between your rounds and have to redo your stitches to make it tighter, then using the magic circle way is to do it. All you do is make an adjustable chain and pull the yarn tail to tighten it as much as you like. Whenever you are crocheting a motif, make sure to choose one way and stick with it all the way.

Use the Same Sized Hook for Your Chain as You Use For the Entire Project

The most essential tool you will need for crocheting your projects is a crochet hook. They come in all different sizes, materials, and types. As a beginner, you might think that all hooks work the same way. However, choosing the wrong hook size can drastically change the look of your project. Every pattern you choose has a specific hook size written in the instruction, and making a change in that will make your stitch either too tight or too loose. So pay extra attention to the pattern instruction to make sure you are using the right-sized hook. Making a gauge swatch can help you when you accidentally use the wrong hook size and save you from wasting a lot of time. So if your stitches seem a little too tight, try switching up your hook size, and if your stitches are coming off looser than you want, then choose a smaller hook.

Shrinking or Growing Crochet

You are working on your project, and suddenly, you notice that something is wrong. If you notice your project slowly growing or slowly shrinking, that means that you are doing something wrong. First, check if you are using the right hook size, as you learned in the previous heading, then check if you are putting the first stitch in the right spot. Putting your stitch in the wrong place can make your square turn into a triangle. Before you move on, it is important to learn how to start your first stitch after you are done with your foundation chain. If you are using a single crochet stitch, then your first stitch should go into the first stitch of the foundation chain. And if you are using any of the other basic stitches, then the turning chain will count as your first stitch, so the stitch you are working on will go into the second stitch of your previously done row.

Trusting the Manufacturers' Knots

We all know how frustrating it is to unwind and rewind your yarn hank into a ball, so we mostly try to opt for ready-made yarn balls, which makes our work easier. However, sadly most of the time, you will find at least one or sometimes two knots in your yarn ball. We often just let it go and continue crocheting using it as it is. What you do not know is that these knots can sometimes come apart and ruin your hard work. So, my advice is to never trust the knots made by manufacturer's they are machine made, so they can easily come off when you least expect it. The best thing you could do with this knot is to first cut it out before you continue crocheting, then rejoin it using the Russian join you learned in the previous chapter. This will secure the knot can make sure your yarn does not come off mid-project.

Not Knowing About Yarn Quality

As a beginner, we often get indulged in buying pretty, multicolored, fluffy, or dark yarn, which can make it harder for you to count your stitches or work with in general. In the beginning, you might be tempted to buy something cool looking or inexpensive because you do not want to risk getting expensive yarn if you are not sure how committed you will be to this craft. However, bad-quality yarn can make your crochet experience worse, cheap acrylics will feel rough and squeaky, and they will not drape well in your hands while crocheting. This can make you dread even starting your project. So, before you buy any yarn, make sure to check online and learn about the best-recommended yarns for beginners. Personally, I think yarn that is lighter and made of natural fibers is perfect for beginners as it is easier to work with, and stitches are way neater compared to mixed acrylics or fluffy yarn. This makes it easier for you to notice and correct any mistakes while working on your projects.

Not Knowing About C2C

Many of you must have heard the term C2C; it is an abbreviation of corner-to-corner which is a crochet technique used to work diagonally in blocks made of three chains and three double crochets that you will join with a slip stitch. In other words, you will create little squares that will be connected and work from corner to corner. The crochet blocks will get stitched using a slip stitch to three chain spaces from the previous row, and an increase will be made until the width you want is achieved. After you achieve your desired width, you will decrease the project back down, and to estimate the number of corner-to-corner squares; you have to use a C2C calculator. This technique is often used to make blankets as they are the perfect example of square projects. You can also use a grid of squares to help you identify where you are in the pattern if you feel like you have lost count of your stitches and will let you know if there are any color changes or any stitches that you need to finish your project.

Not Knowing How to Crochet in Rounds

At the beginning of your crochet journey, you will learn about many patterns that work on flat fabrics. These are common to work on when you first start crocheting. However, when you start exploring more projects, you will hear the phrase join the round very often; it can seem confusing at first because it involves a different way of moving onto the next row compared to when working on flat patterns. When I first started crocheting, I often joined and ended my round in the wrong stitch, which threw my stitch count out of the track, and the entire pattern would look weird. However, you can easily fix this by redoing the joining and ending of your round. The first step to learning how to correctly crochet in rounds is to learn how to first join a chain of stitches to join your project in the round. After finishing your first row, make sure your chain is not twisted; it is easier for your chain strand to get tangled up when you join it in the round.

So first, lay your finished row of chain stitches in a round how you want it to look and get rid of any twists that may happen, then join it using a slip stitch. Sometimes patterns might not work in continuous rounds, so you will have to join your row together in a round. To make sure you do not join your rounds in the wrong stitch, try using stitch markers to mark the beginning of your row where you want the join to end. And stop 2 stitches before because you already left them at the beginning of your row, then join your completed row using a slip stitch into the first two stitches to complete to round. It can take some time to process this information easily while crocheting; however, keep practicing till you get the hang of it!

Not Knowing How to Weave in Ends the Right Way

Weaving in the ends of your crochet project is crucial in ensuring that your work stays intact over time. However, if you do not weave in the ends correctly, it can cause your project to become unraveled or come apart at the seams. One mistake that beginners often make when weaving in the ends is not weaving them in far enough. It can be tempting to simply weave the ends in and clip them close to work, but this can cause the ends to come loose over time. To properly secure your ends, you should weave them in for at least two inches, making sure to follow the direction of your stitches. This will help lock the yarn and prevent it from unraveling. There are several different methods for weaving in ends, and some are more effective than others. One common technique is to weave the ends through the back of your stitches, working back and forth until the yarn is secure. Another technique is to use a darning needle to sew the ends into the fabric, creating a seamless finish. Choosing the right technique to weave your ends depends on your personal preference for how you want the finished project to look. For example, if you are working with a slippery or delicate yarn, you may need to take extra care to ensure that the ends are properly secured. Likewise, suppose you are working on a project with a lot of tension or stress, such as a blanket or sweater. In that case, you may want to use a more robust weaving-in technique to ensure that the ends do not come loose over time.

Not Counting Your Rows

Many crochet patterns you find online or in guidebooks will tell you the number of stitches you need in a row in brackets and exactly how many rows you are required to crochet to do your project. Usually, it is easy to count rows; it depends on your pattern and stitches as well if you look closely. Try to keep count as you progress through your project to help avoid any errors when you finish your work. You can make it easy for yourself by keeping a pen and notepad nearby or within your crochet bag to help keep a record of the number of stitches and rows you have completed so far. Stitch markers are also a great tool that can help you in keeping a count of your regular intervals by placing one after every 10 or 20 stitches. Many times when you are crocheting an easy stitch and slowly zone out while crocheting, you will find yourself in the middle of 5 extra rows that were not required for the project. You can also use row counters which we discussed in the previous chapters, which are excellent tools for helping you count your rows. There are many different kinds of row counters in the market these days, so grab the one that you prefer and get back to crocheting.

Not Counting the Starting Chain Correctly or Where to Put the First Stitch

A very newbie mistake that most beginners make is not understanding how to correctly count their starting or foundation chain or know where to put that first stitch. The basic stitch you will learn at the beginning will be the chain stitch you use to build your project. It can be confusing to understand where to put your first stitch after you are done crocheting a foundation chain of stitches. Many beginners find themselves in a turmoil of mistakes after they cannot find where they went wrong when crocheting their fabric. And how a regular-looking square turned into a diamond or triangle. The mistake starts from placing their first stitch wrong; this throws off your entire stitch count and makes your fabric uneven when you compare it to the pattern instructions. So remember that when you are working with a chain, you will always count the first two chains as your first stitch, and the one you correctly working on is the second stitch. So make sure to poke your hook in the right place!

Not Leaving the Yarn Tail Long Enough

One of the most common mistakes that crochet beginners make is not leaving a long enough yarn tail at the beginning or end of their work. This might seem like a minor detail, but it can actually have a significant impact on the success of your project. When you start a new row or switch to a new color, you typically need to tie off the old yarn and begin working with the new yarn. If you do not leave a long enough tail at the end of the old yarn, you might not have enough yarn to properly tie off the stitch. This can cause your work to unravel, leaving a hole in your project or causing your stitches to become misaligned. Additionally, if you do not leave a long enough tail at the beginning or end of your work, it can be difficult to weave in the ends when finished. Weaving in the ends is an important step in finishing your project, as it helps to secure your stitches and prevent the work from unraveling. If you do not have enough yarn to weave in the ends properly, your project may come apart over time.

Chapter 5:
Types of Crochet You Will See in the World

Crochet is a versatile and enjoyable craft that involves creating fabrics and designs by looping yarn or thread with a crochet hook. There are many different types of crochet techniques and projects that you can explore as a beginner or experienced crocheter. Here are some of the main types of crochet to help you get started:

Amigurumi Crochet

Amigurumi crochet is a Japanese crochet technique that involves creating small stuffed animals and other cute creatures like Pokémon. The word "amigurumi" comes from the Japanese words "ami" which means to crochet or knit, and "nuigurumi" which means a stuffed toy. The technique involves using a small crochet hook and fine yarn to create tight, dense stitches, which give the finished project a firm, three-dimensional shape. The crocheter starts by crocheting a series of simple shapes, such as circles, ovals, and spheres, which are then stuffed and sewn together to create the desired animal or character. One thing that makes amigurumi crochet different from other crochet is the use of safety eyes and other small details, such as noses, mouths, and ears, typically made from felt or other materials sewn onto the finished project. The final result is an adorable stuffed toy that could be the perfect gift for your loved ones. You can even add a keychain hook to make it more personalized.

Projects made with this crochet require a certain level of skill and patience to create. The technique involves working with small, tight stitches, which can be challenging for beginners. However, with practice and perseverance, anyone can learn to master the art of amigurumi crochet. In addition to stuffed animals and creatures, amigurumi crochet can be used to create a wide variety of other projects, including key chains, ornaments, and even small bags and purses. The technique is also highly customizable, with endless possibilities for experimenting with different colors, textures, and shapes. So do learn this playful crochet technique to create many adorable projects for yourself and your loved ones!

Aran Crochet

Aran crochet is a style of crochet that is distinguished through its use of complex cable patterns inspired by the traditionally knitted sweaters of the Aran Islands off the west coast of Ireland. This crochet style uses a chunky, textured yarn and a large crochet hook to create a dense, sturdy, warm, cozy fabric. Crochet patterns using this crochet type are used to create crossing stitches over each other to form

braids and other textured motifs. These patterns can range from simple twists and braids to more complex designs and can be worked in a single color or multiple colors to create a beautiful color contrast. The Aran crochet technique has been adapted to create a wide variety of designs, including hats, scarves, sweaters, and even home decor items like blankets and pillows. The most distinctive feature of Aran crochet is its use of texture to create a rich, layered effect. You used to work with a combination of different stitch patterns and textures; this crochet type can be used to create extra depth and dimension to your project that cannot be found in other crochet types. It can be a challenging technique for beginners to master, as it requires a good understanding of basic crochet stitches and techniques and the ability to read and follow complex pattern instructions. However, with practice and perseverance, anyone can learn to create beautiful Aran crochet designs.

Bavarian Crochet

This is a crochet style that originated in Bavaria, Germany. It is known for its use of bold, geometric shapes and rich, textured fabrics. Unlike other types of crochet, Bavarian crochet is worked in rounds, using a series of increasing and decreasing stitches to create a spiral

pattern. The stitch pattern is made up of a combination of double crochet, chain stitches, and slip stitches, which are used to create the beautiful interlocking motifs characteristic of this style. One of the defining features of this crochet is its use of color, with many traditional Bavarian designs featuring bold, contrasting colors that create a striking visual impact. This makes Bavarian a perfect choice for creating personalized accessories like scarves, hats, and bags. One of the good things about Bavarian is its flexibility, as the stitch pattern can be adapted to create a wide variety of different designs and motifs.

Bullion Crochet

Bullion crochet is a unique crochet technique that is used to create textured, raised stitches that resemble coiled ropes or vines. The stitch is created by wrapping the yarn multiple times around the crochet hook to form a tight spiral, which is then pulled through a loop on the previous row to create the finished stitch. Bullion crochet can be used to create a variety of different designs and patterns, including flowers, leaves, and other decorative elements. The technique is often combined with other crochet stitches to create neat and detailed designs that can be used to create flat and three-dimensional objects. One

of the main challenges of bullion crochet is mastering the technique of creating the tight spirals that form the basis of the stitch. It requires a combination of precision and patience to wrap the yarn tightly enough around the hook without letting it slip or become too loose. However, with practice and perseverance, anyone can master this technique and create beautiful and unique designs. It is commonly used due to its versatility, which can help you to create a delicate and lacy design or a bold and textured motif; bullion crochet is a technique that can help you achieve your creative vision.

Broomstick Crochet

Broomstick crochet is a unique form of crochet that involves using a large knitting needle or broomstick as an additional tool to create loops that are larger compared to those made with just a crochet hook. You start by making a foundation of chain using your regular crochet hook, then insert a large knitting needle or broomstick through the loops of the foundation chain to create larger loops that will be used to make the stitches. You then work a series of stitches into the larger loops you have created to end up making a lacy and open design. The use of a broomstick is what gives this crochet its unique name,

distinctive texture, and appearance. The size of the tool can be varied to create different effects, with larger tools creating larger loops and a more open, airy design, while smaller tools create tighter, denser stitches. Broomstick crochet can create a wide range of projects, including scarves, shawls, blankets, and even clothing items like sweaters and dresses. The open, lacy design makes it especially well-suited for warm-weather items, as it allows air to circulate and keeps the wearer cool. One of the challenges of broomstick crochet is learning to control the tension of the larger loops created by the tool. Maintaining even tension throughout the project can be tricky, and it may take some practice to achieve the desired results. However, you can create unique and beautiful crochet designs once the technique is mastered.

Bruges Crochet

Bruges crochet is a lace-making technique that originated in Belgium in the late 19th century. It is created using a combination of openwork and textured stitches, creating a delicate, lacy fabric with a distinctive, three-dimensional appearance. The technique of Bruges crochet involves working in rows of open mesh stitches, with each row being joined to the previous row with decorative loops or chains.

These loops create a lacy, openwork pattern that is often accented with textured stitches such as bobbles or picots. One of the unique features of this crochet type is the use of shaping to create decorative motifs. This can include scalloped edges, curved shapes, and even three-dimensional objects like flowers or butterflies. Shaping is achieved through a combination of increases and decreases in the number of stitches worked in each row, as well as the use of chains and loops to create the desired shape. It is often worked using fine, lightweight yarns or threads and small crochet hooks to achieve the delicate, lacy texture of the fabric. It can be used to create a wide range of projects, including doilies, tablecloths, and even clothing items like blouses or skirts.

Clothesline Crochet

Clothesline crochet is another unique technique involving incorporating a clothesline or cord into the stitches. This gives the finished fabric a sturdy, three-dimensional texture that can be used to create a wide range of functional and decorative items. To use clothesline crochet, you will first take a sturdy cord or clothesline and wrap it with a thin, flexible yarn or string, creating the base or core for the crochet stitches to be worked around. The cord can be wrapped in a

variety of colors to create a striped or patterned effect. Once the cord is wrapped, you can begin working stitches around the cord. The most common stitch used in this type is the single crochet stitch, which is worked around the cord to create a tight, durable fabric. This crochet can be used to create a variety of items, from functional home decor like baskets and rugs to fashionable accessories like handbags and belts. The technique can be adapted to suit a wide range of styles and projects and is often combined with other crochet techniques like texture stitches to create unique and eye-catching designs. It can be a bit challenging compared to traditional crochet techniques due to the bulk of the cord; it is a fun way to experiment with different materials and textures in your crochet projects.

Clones Lace Crochet

Clones Lace Crochet is a traditional form of Irish lace crochet that originated in the mid-19th century in Clones, County Monaghan, Ireland. It is an extremely detailed form of crochet that is often used to create delicate decorative items such as lace doilies or table runners. The technique involves working with very fine crochet thread and a tiny hook, typically around a size of 0.5mm. The stitches used

in this crochet include chain stitches, single crochet stitches, and double crochet stitches. However, you work with them tightly to create a dense and textured fabric. The unique feature of this crochet is the use of decorative motifs that are created using a combination of simple stitches and more complex techniques like picots, bullion stitches, and clusters. The patterns often include floral motifs, leaves, and other delicate designs. Clones Lace Crochet is known for its beauty and the skill required to create it. Many of the traditional Clones Lace Crochet patterns are passed down through families and communities and are still being used and adapted by other crocheters.

Cro-Hook Crochet

Cro Hook crochet, also known as double-ended crochet. It is a type of crochet that combines techniques of both crochet and knitting. It is done using a special double-ended crochet hook that has a hook on each end. The cro-hook technique involves working two separate strands of yarn at the same time, one with each hook of the double-ended crochet hook. The fabric created with this technique has a distinctive texture and appearance, often resembling a knit fabric but with crochet's added texture and detail. One of the advantages of

Cro Hook crochet is the ability to create complex color patterns and textures without the need for complicated color changes. By working with two strands of yarn at once, crocheters can create stripes, ombre effects, and other color patterns without cutting and weaving in multiple ends of yarn. This technique can be a little complicated for beginners; however, the result makes it worth the trouble, making it popular amongst many crocheters.

Filet Crochet

Filet crochet is a technique that involves creating a lacy, mesh-like fabric with a grid-like structure of open and closed spaces. The fabric created with this technique is used for both decorative and functional items such as tablecloths, curtains, and doilies. Filet crochet is typically worked with a single color of yarn using a small hook and a chart or pattern. The chart or pattern represents the design that will be created, with each square on the chart representing a stitch in the pattern. To create the unique stitches used in the filet crochet fabric, crocheters work a combination of double crochet stitches and chain stitches. The double crochet stitches create solid blocks of fabric, while the chain stitches create open spaces. The pattern is worked

by alternating between the two stitches, following the chart or pattern to create the desired design. In addition to traditional charts and patterns, filet crochet can also be worked with custom designs created by the crocheter. By creating a chart or pattern that represents the desired design, crocheters can create custom filet crochet pieces that are uniquely their own.

Finger Crochet

Finger crochet is a special technique that does not require the use of a crochet hook; instead, the crocheter uses only their fingers to create crochet stitches. This method of crocheting is particularly popular among kids and beginners who are still learning how to use a hook. The finger crochet technique involves wrapping the yarn around the fingers to create loops and then pulling the loops through each other to form stitches. To begin, the yarn is wrapped around the index finger, with the tail end held in the palm. The yarn is then wrapped around the index finger again, creating a loop on the finger. Then, the loop is pulled through the first loop, creating a chain stitch. To create the next stitch, the yarn is wrapped around the index finger again, and a new loop is pulled through the previous loop. This process is repeated,

with the crocheter using their other fingers to help hold the loops in place. The size of the stitches can be adjusted by changing the size of the loops created on the fingers. The resulting fabric has a loose, open texture that is perfect for lightweight and airy garments. Finger crochet is a fun and easy way to create crochet projects without the need for a hook, making it accessible to all ages and skill levels. It can also be a great way to use up yarn scraps or try out new stitch patterns before committing to a larger project with a hook. With a little practice, finger crochet can be a valuable addition to any crocheter's skillset.

Freeform Crochet

Freeform crochet is a type of crochet with no set patterns or rules to follow, giving the artist complete creative freedom to create whatever they desire. The technique also involves stitching together various pieces of crochet work to form a larger design. Freeform crochet has no specific structure or shape to follow, allowing the crocheter to follow their imagination and creativity. Freeform crochet projects often feature bold colors, various textures, and interesting shapes that come together uniquely and beautifully. This type of crochet is particularly popular among artists and designers who enjoy creating art pieces or wearable accessories that showcase their individual style and artistic flair. Some freeform crochet

projects include colorful blankets, unique clothing pieces, and one-of-a-kind wall hangings. Artists typically start with a basic shape or foundation piece, such as a square or rectangle, to begin a freeform crochet project. From there, they begin to add additional stitches and pieces to create a unique and personalized design. You can use any type, weight, or color of yarn in your project, which makes it perfect for people who like doing personalized projects without any guidelines.

Hairpin Crochet

Hairpin crochet, as the name states, involves the use of a special tool known as a hairpin loom or a hairpin lace loom. This tool consists of two parallel metal rods joined together at the top and bottom by a crosspiece, with a small space between the rods. Hairpin crochet is often used to create lace-like designs that have a delicate appearance. To begin a crochet project using this type of crochet, you will first start by creating a length of loops on the hairpin loom. This is done by wrapping yarn around the two parallel rods of the loom, creating a chain-like series of loops that can be adjusted to the desired length. Once the loops have been created, the actual crocheting can begin. The crocheting is done using a crochet hook to work stitches through the loops on the hairpin loom. One common stitch used in

hairpin crochet is the single crochet stitch, which is worked by inserting the hook through a loop on one side of the loom, then through a loop on the opposite side, drawing the yarn through both loops to create a stitch. Other common stitches used in hairpin crochet include double and treble crochet. One of the benefits of this crochet type is the ability to create different designs and patterns using only a few stitches. By using different heights and placement of stitches, you can make a variety of textures and patterns. Some hairpin crochet designs also incorporate beads or other embellishments, adding further interest to the finished product. Hairpin crochet can be used to create a wide range of projects, from delicate lace doilies and shawls to sturdy Afghans and blankets. It is also popular for creating edgings and trims on other crochet projects, such as scarves and hats. While hairpin crochet can take some practice to master, the results can be well worth the effort of creating beautiful and unique crochet designs.

Micro Crochet

Micro crochet is a type of crochet that involves using very fine thread and tiny hooks to create intricate designs and patterns. It is used to create delicate items such as miniature dollhouse furniture, jewelry, and lace. The term "micro crochet" refers to the small size of the

hooks and thread used, typically ranging from 0.4mm to 1.5mm in hook size and thread weights of 80-200. Because of the small size, micro crochet requires a great deal of patience, precision, good eyesight, and dexterity. Micro crochet techniques can vary depending on the desired outcome, but some common methods include single crochet, double crochet, and slip stitch. The key is to work slowly and carefully, making small, evenly spaced, and tightly worked stitches. You can usually find the creation of miniature food items using this crochet, such as tiny crochet fruits, junk food, and veggies, which are used as decorations for larger projects such as a doll house.

Overlay Crochet

Overlay crochet is a technique that involves layering one or more crochet motifs over a base fabric or background. This technique creates a three-dimensional effect that makes the design pop and adds depth to the finished project. To create a project using overlay crochet,

you will start by crocheting a base fabric or background in a solid color. They then work a series of crochet motifs in a contrasting color, which are then sewn or crocheted onto the base fabric. The motifs used in overlay crochet can be simple or complex, ranging from geometric shapes to intricate floral patterns. Some overlay crochet projects use multiple layers of motifs, creating a multi-dimensional effect that adds depth and texture to the design. One great thing about this crochet type is that it allows crafters to create highly detailed and intricate designs with a level of precision that is difficult to achieve with other crochet techniques. It also allows for great creativity and flexibility, as the crafter can experiment with different colors, textures, and motifs to create unique and personalized designs.

Pineapple Crochet

Pineapple crochet is a type of crochet that features lacy motifs resembling pineapples. These motifs are typically worked in rounds or rows and can be combined to create a wide variety of projects, from doilies and table runners to shawls, blankets, and even clothing. The

pineapple motif itself is made up of a series of shells, each consisting of several double crochet stitches worked together. These shells are then separated by chains, creating spaces between the pineapple sections. To work a pineapple motif, the crafter typically begins with a small circle or square, forming the motif's center. From there, they work a series of shells and chains, increasing the number of stitches in each shell to create the distinctive shape of the pineapple. As the motif grows larger, you may need to add additional rounds of shells and chains to maintain the shape and balance of the design. Once the motif is complete, it can be used on its own as a decorative element or combined with other motifs to create a larger project. It is a popular technique among those who enjoy creating delicate, lacy designs with intricate detail. The technique is often used to create heirloom-quality pieces that are cherished for their beauty and craftsmanship. This crochet is liked amongst crocheters because it can be worked in a wide variety of yarns and colors, allowing you to create designs that are uniquely their own. With a little practice and patience, anyone can learn to master the art of pineapple crochet and create stunning works of art.

Stained Glass Crochet

Stained glass crochet is a type of crochet that is used to create the look of stained glass windows in a textile format. This technique involves using colored yarns to create blocks of color, bordered with black or dark yarn, to create the look of stained glass leading. To start a project using stained glass crochet, you must first select a pattern or design made up of blocks of color. The blocks are typically worked in a combination of single crochet and double crochet stitches, with each color being worked in rows or rounds to create a solid block of color. Once the blocks of color are complete, the crafter adds the "leading" by working a round of single crochet stitches around each block in black or dark yarn. This creates the look of leading between the colored blocks, just like in a stained glass window. It can be used to create a wide variety of projects, from simple coasters and placemats to more complex designs like blankets, wall hangings, and even clothing. The technique is particularly popular among those who enjoy working with color and creating bold graphic designs. Crocheters love this technique because it allows them to create complex designs without worrying about having to carry multiple yarns at once. Each crocheted block of color is worked separately, and the black leading creates a clean, finished edge between the blocks.

Symbol Crochet

Symbol crochet, also known as diagram or chart crochet, is a type of crochet that uses graphic symbols to represent each stitch of a pattern. These symbols are typically presented in a chart or diagram, allowing the crafter to see the entire pattern and work more efficiently. This type of crochet is particularly useful for complex or intricate patterns, as it can be difficult to read written instructions for every stitch. With the symbol crochet, the crafter can quickly and easily understand the pattern by referring to the chart. Each symbol represents a specific stitch or group of stitches. The chart will typically include a legend explaining what each symbol means. Common symbols include squares or circles representing single-crochet or double-crochet stitches and diagonal lines or arrows representing increases or decreases. To work a pattern in symbol crochet, the crafter follows the chart row by row, working each stitch as indicated by the symbol. The chart may include additional information, such as stitch counts, color changes, and special instructions. This type of crochet is a popular technique in many parts of the world, particularly in Eastern Europe and Asia. It is used to create complex lace patterns, as well as pictorial designs that feature images or symbols.

Tapestry Crochet

Tapestry crochet is a type of crochet that is used to create intricate designs and patterns using multiple colors of yarn. This technique involves carrying two or more colors of yarn at once, and working stitches over the unused colors to create a woven, tapestry-like effect. To begin, the crafter selects a pattern or design to create, and charts out the colors and stitches needed to complete the design. The pattern is typically worked in single crochet stitches, but other stitches, such as half-double crochet or double crochet, can also be used. As the crafter works the design, they carry the unused yarns along the back of the work, weaving them over and under the stitches of the current row. When a color change is needed, the new color is picked up and worked over the old color, trapping it in place. One of the challenges of tapestry crochet is maintaining an even tension throughout the work. The unused yarns must be carried loosely enough to allow the stitches to lay flat but not so loosely that they create holes or gaps in the work. Tapestry crochet can be used to create a wide range of projects, from simple coasters and mug rugs to more complex designs like blankets, bags, and even clothing. The technique is particularly popular in South America and Africa, where it has been used for centuries to create beautiful and functional textiles.

Tunisian Crochet

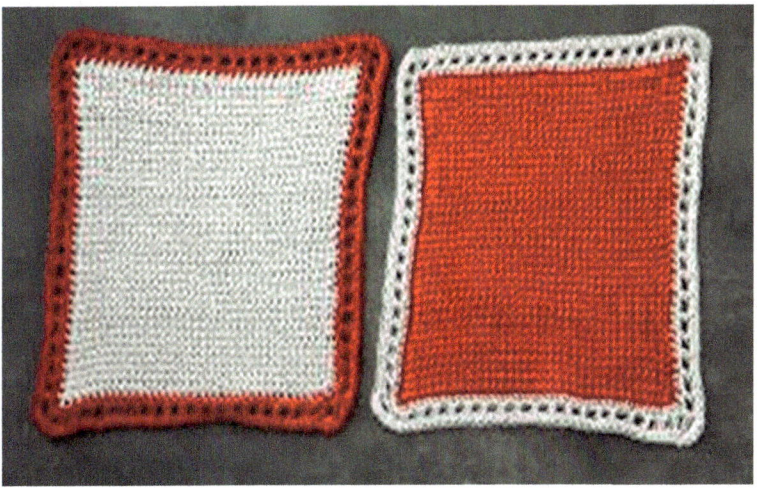

Tunisian crochet, also known as Afghan crochet, uses an elongated hook and a unique stitch to create a fabric that resembles knitting. Tunisian crochet produces a dense and sturdy fabric with a distinctive vertical texture that is ideal for creating blankets, scarves, and other warm and cozy items. This technique involves holding a long crochet hook, typically with a stopper on the end, to prevent stitches from falling off. The crafter works with a large number of loops on the hook at once, creating a row of stitches that resembles knitting. Tunisian crochet combines traditional crochet stitches, like the chain stitch and single crochet, with its own unique stitches, such as the Tunisian simple stitch and Tunisian knit stitch. The Tunisian simple stitch, the foundation of Tunisian crochet, produces a fabric with a distinctive vertical texture. To work this stitch, you insert the hook through the front loop of the previous row's stitch, yarn over, and pull through to create a new loop, repeating this process across the row. On the other hand, the Tunisian knit stitch mimics the appearance of knitted stockinette fabric. This stitch is worked by inserting the hook between two stitches of the previous row, yarning over, and pulling through to form a new loop, again repeating the process across the row. Tunisian crochet can be worked in various ways, including in the round or flat rows. It also offers versatility for creating different stitches and patterns, such as cables, lace, and colorwork.

Chapter 6:
Let's Start Crocheting!

In this last chapter, you will learn about some beginner-friendly crochet projects that will allow you to put your new skills into practice. These projects are designed to be straightforward, with step-by-step instructions to help guide you through each step. We all understand that starting a new craft can be overwhelming, which is why I have chosen projects that are both easy to make and practical to use. From cozy scarves and hats to practical dishcloths and baby blankets, each project is designed to build your confidence and help you master the basics of crochet. However, even though these projects are simple, they are far from boring. You will learn how to combine different stitch patterns and colors to create unique textures and designs. And you can easily adapt these projects to suit your style and preferences.

Whether you are doing these projects for yourself or as gifts for friends and family, I hope they will inspire you to continue your crochet journey and explore all the possibilities that this wonderful craft has to offer. So, grab your hook and yarn, and let's get started on these fun and easy beginner projects.

Beginners Crochet Washcloths

Crochet washcloths are a perfect beginner project that can be completed quickly and easily. Not only are they practical, but they also make a great addition to any bathroom decor. The beauty of crochet washcloths is that they can be customized to suit your personal preferences. You can choose your colors and stitch patterns to create a unique and personalized washcloth that is perfect for your bathroom or as a gift for a loved one.

So, if you are looking for a quick and easy project or a beginner just starting, this washcloth project is the perfect way to get started on your crochet journey. Let's get started and create something beautiful and functional. Here is an easy tutorial on how to crochet a washcloth for beginners:

Materials

- Cotton mixed fiber yarn of any color of choice
- Crochet hook (size H/5mm is recommended)

- Scissors
- Tapestry needle

Instructions

- Make a slipknot and chain 26 stitches.
- Start from the second chain on your hook and make a stitch using a single crochet. Then, continue to make it into each chain until the end of the row.
- In the first chain, then rotate your work from one side to the other. Then, in the first stitch of the previous row, make another single crochet, then continue to make it into each stitch across the row.
- Repeat step 3 until your washcloth measures approximately 8 inches in length. This should be about 24 rows; however, you can adjust the length to your desired preference.
- To finish off your washcloth, cut the yarn leaving a long tail of about 6 inches. Pull the tail end through the last loop on your hook and weave it in using a tapestry needle.
- To create a neat border, you can single crochet around the edges of your washcloth. Starting at any corner, attach your yarn and single crochet evenly around the washcloth, making 3 single crochets in each corner. Make a slip stitch into the first single crochet to join when you reach the start.
- Cut the yarn and weave it in the ends using a tapestry needle.

Your crochet washcloth is now complete! You can use it in the bath or shower or even as a dishcloth in the kitchen. You can make several washcloths in different colors to match your decor or as gifts for family and friends.

Beginners Crochet Scarf

A crochet scarf is a classic project that is perfect for beginners looking to take their crochet skills to the next level. Scarves are a practical and stylish accessory for the colder months that can add to the style factor of any good outfit. You will be provided with step-by-step instructions to guide you through the process of creating your scarf. It's simple, quick, and practical and allows you to practice basic stitches and techniques. So let's get crocheting a simple crochet scarf for beginners!

Materials:

- Worsted weight yarn (in the color of choice)
- Crochet hook (size H/5mm is recommended)
- Scissors
- Tapestry needle

Instructions:

- Make a slipknot and chain 20 stitches.
- Do a double crochet stitch into the fourth chain from your crochet hook. Then, double crochet into each chain and stitch across the row.

- Chain 3, then rotate your work from one side to the other around. Double crochet into the first stitch of the previous row, then continue to make a double crochet stitch into each stitch across the row.
- Repeat these steps until your scarf is the desired length. This can vary depending on your preference, but a typical scarf length is around 60-70 inches.
- To finish off your scarf, cut the yarn leaving a tail of about 6 inches. Pull the tail through the last loop on your hook and weave it in using a tapestry needle.
- To create a neat border, you can single crochet around the edges of your scarf. Starting at any corner, attach your yarn and single crochet evenly around the scarf, making 3 single crochets in each corner. When you reach the start, make a slip stitch into the first single crochet to join it.
- Cut the yarn and weave it in the ends using a tapestry needle.

Your crochet scarf is now complete! You can wear it in different ways, such as wrapping it around your neck or letting it hang loose. You can make several scarves in different colors to match your outfits or as gifts for family and friends. Crocheting a scarf is a great way to practice basic stitches and techniques while creating a useful and practical item. With a little practice, you can make a variety of scarves in different sizes and colors, and even experiment with more complex stitch patterns.

Bobble Headband

If you are looking for a fun and trendy crochet project, a bobble headband is the perfect place to start! This project is quick and easy to make, and it also serves as a stylish accessory for any season. The beauty of crochet headbands is that they can be customized to suit your personal style. You can choose your colors and stitch patterns to create a unique and personalized headband that is perfect for your wardrobe. Crocheting a bobble stitch headband is a fun and unique

project for beginners. It's a great way to practice the bobble stitch and create a stylish accessory. Following is a step-by-step tutorial on how to crochet a bobble stitch headband for beginners:

Materials:

- Worsted weight yarn in the color of your choice
- Crochet hook (size H/5mm is recommended)
- Scissors
- Tapestry needle

Instructions:

- Make a slipknot and chain 18 stitches.
- Do a double crochet stitch into the third chain from your crochet hook. Then, double crochet stitches into each chain stitch across the row.
- In the second chain, then rotate your work from one side to the other. Double crochet into the first stitch of the previous row. Then, make a complete bobble stitch as you have learned in the previous chapter about stitch variations, then make

another double crochet into the next stitch. Repeat this pattern of changing between bobble stitch and double crochet stitch across the row.
- In the second chain, then rotate your work from one side to the other. Double crochet into the first stitch of the previous row. Double crochet into each stitch across the row.
- Repeat step 3 to create another row of bobble stitches, followed by a row of double crochet stitches.
- Repeat steps 4 and 5 until your headband is the desired length. This can vary depending on your preference, but a typical headband length is around 20-22 inches.
- To finish off your headband, cut the yarn leaving a tail of about 6 inches. Pull the tail through the last loop on your hook and weave it in using a tapestry needle.
- To create a neat border, you can single crochet around the edges of your headband. Starting at any corner, attach your yarn and single crochet evenly around the headband, making 3 single crochets in each corner. When you reach the start, use a slip stitch to join it with the first single crochet.
- Cut the yarn and weave it in the ends using a tapestry needle.

Your crochet bobble stitch headband is now complete! You can wear it to warm your ears during chilly weather or as a stylish accessory. You can make several headbands in different colors to match your outfits. Crocheting a bobble stitch headband is a great way to practice the bobble stitch and create a unique and stylish accessory. With a little practice, you can experiment with different colors and yarn types to create a variety of headbands.

Classic Granny Squares

Granny squares are one of the most iconic and versatile crochet motifs, and they make for a great beginner project. With just a few basic crochet stitches and some yarn, you can create beautiful and unique squares that can be used for a variety of projects, from blankets

to scarves to bags and more. You will learn how to crochet a granny square with easy-to-follow instructions that will guide you through each step of the process, from creating the center ring to working the clusters of stitches that give the granny square its signature look. And once you have mastered the basic granny square, you can easily learn how to join multiple squares together to create a larger project. You will also learn some fun and creative ways to personalize your granny squares with different color schemes and stitch variations. Not only is the classic granny square project a great way to hone your crochet skills, but it is also a fun and satisfying project that you can work on over time. With each square you complete, you will see your project grow and take shape. Now, all you have to do is follow this step-by-step tutorial on how to crochet a classic granny square for beginners:

Materials:

- Worsted weight yarn in at least 2 colors
- Crochet hook (size H/5mm is recommended)
- Scissors
- Tapestry needle

Instructions:

- Make a slipknot and chain 4 stitches. Then, make a slip stitch into your first chain to form a loop.
- In the third chain, make 2 double crochet stitches into the center of the loop. In the second chain, then make 3 double crochet stitches into the center of the loop. This forms the first shell of your granny square.
- In the second chain, then make 3 double crochets into the center of the loop. In the second chain, then make 3 double crochets into the center of the loop. This forms the second shell of your granny square.
- Repeat step 3 until you have four shells in total. In the second chain, then slip stitch into the top of the first chain to join.
- Cut the yarn and weave in the tail ends using a tapestry needle.
- To start the next round, all you need to do is attach a new color of yarn to any corner chain-2 space. In the third chain, make 2 double crochets into the same chain-2 space. In the second chain, then make 3 double crochets into the same chain-2 space. This forms the first corner of your granny square.
- In the first chain, then make 3 double crochets into the next chain-2 space. In the second chain, make 3 double crochets into the same chain-2 space. This forms the next corner of your granny square.
- Repeat step 7 for each chain-2 space around the square, making sure to chain one in between each shell.
- In the second chain, make a slip stitch into the top of the first chain to join.
- Cut the yarn and weave in the tail ends using a tapestry needle.
- To add more rounds, repeat steps from the last round you made, and make sure to add a chain-2 space and shell in each corner and chaining 1 in between each shell.
- Once your granny square is the desired size, finish off the last round and weave in the ends using a tapestry needle.

Your classic granny square is now complete! You can use it as a base for other projects or make multiple squares to join together into a larger project like a blanket or scarf. Experiment with different colors and yarn types to create a unique and personalized granny square project.

Beanie

Beanies are a staple accessory for any wardrobe, and crocheting your own is a fun and rewarding way to personalize your style. Whether you are new to crochet or looking to expand your skills, this beanie project is a great way to hone your techniques while creating a cozy and stylish accessory. Crocheting a basic beanie hat is a great project for beginners to learn and practice the basic stitches and techniques of crochet. So, follow this step-by-step tutorial on how to crochet a basic beanie hat for beginners:

Materials:

- Worsted weight yarn in any color (approx. 100-150g)

- Crochet hook (size H/5mm is recommended)
- Scissors
- Tapestry needle

Instructions:

- Make a slipknot and chain 4 stitches. Then, form a loop using a slip stitch into the first chain.
- In the second chain, then make 11 double crochet stitches into the center of the loop. Then, join into the top of the first chain using a slip stitch.
- In the second chain, then make 2 double crochet stitches into each stitch around. Then, join into the top of the first chain using a slip stitch.
- In the second chain, then make 1 double crochet into the next stitch and 2 double crochet stitches into the next stitch around. Then, join into the top of the first chain using a slip stitch.
- Then, repeat the last step you did by making 1 double crochet and then 2 double crochet stitches, and lastly, using a slip stitch to join.
- Continue to increase by adding another double crochet stitch between the increases of each round until your beanie hat reaches the desired size. To make sure the size is accurate, try it on periodically as you go.
- Once your beanie hat is the desired size, continue crocheting without increasing it until the hat is the desired length. The length of a traditional beanie hat should be about 7-8 inches.
- To finish the hat, cut the yarn and leave a long tail end of about 12 inches. Then, thread the tail end onto your tapestry needle and weave it through the remaining stitches, pulling tight to close the top of the hat.
- Turn the hat inside out and weave in the tail ends using your tapestry needle.

Your basic crochet beanie hat is now complete! You can experiment with different yarns, colors, and embellishments to create a variety of hats to match your personal style. Happy crocheting!

Scrunchie

Crochet scrunchies are a quick and easy project that can add a fun and playful touch to any hairstyle. Crocheting a basic scrunchie is a fun and easy project for beginners. So follow this step-by-step tutorial on how to crochet a basic scrunchie:

Materials:

- Worsted weight yarn in the color of choice
- Crochet hook (size G/4mm is recommended)
- Hair elastic
- Scissors
- Tapestry needle

Instructions:

- Make a slipknot and chain 6 stitches.
- Then, form a loop by making a slip stitch into the first chain.

- In the first chain, then make 12 single crochets in the center of the loop. Then, join into the top of the first chain using a slip stitch.
- In the first chain, then make 2 single crochets into each stitch around. Then, join into the top of the first chain using a slip stitch.
- In the first chain, then make 1 single crochet into each stitch around. Then, join into the top of the first chain using a slip stitch.
- Repeat step 5 until your scrunchie is the desired width. You will have to crochet about 30-40 rows to make a standard-sized scrunchie.
- Once your scrunchie reaches the desired width, cut the yarn end and leave a long tail end of about 12 inches.
- Thread the yarn tail onto your tapestry needle and weave it through the stitches of the last row. Pull tight to cinch the scrunchie closed.
- Secure the yarn by knotting it a few times and then trim off the excess yarn.
- Take the hair elastic and place it inside the created scrunchie. Tie the two ends of the elastic with a knot, ensuring the knot is secure.
- Lastly, using the tapestry needle, weave in the remaining yarn ends.

Your basic crochet scrunchie is now complete! You can experiment with different yarns and colors to create a variety of scrunchies to match your personal style.

Baby Blanket

Crocheting a baby blanket is a wonderful way to create a cozy and comforting item for a new arrival. One of the great things about this baby blanket project is that it can be customized to suit your personal style. You can choose your own colors and stitch patterns to create a

unique and personalized blanket that is perfect for a new baby or as a gift for a friend or family member. This project is fun and rewarding to make, and it also serves as a great way to practice your crochet skills. You will get plenty of practice with basic stitches like single and double crochets, as well as some more advanced techniques like changing colors and creating texture. Crocheting a baby blanket is a great project for practice using single crochet and half double crochet stitches for beginners. So, follow along with the step-by-step tutorial on how to crochet a baby blanket using these stitches:

Materials:

- Worsted weight yarn in the color of choice
- Crochet hook (size H/5mm is recommended)
- Scissors
- Tapestry needle

Instructions:

- Make a slipknot and chain 100 stitches or until you reach your desired width. Then, start from the second chain into your crochet hook and make a single crochet stitch.
- And then, into each chain across the row, keep making a single crochet stitch.

- In the second chain, rotate your work from one side to the other. Then, make a half-double crochet stitch into the second stitch from the hook and repeat making it into each stitch across the row.
- In the first chain, rotate your work from one side to the other. Then, make a single crochet stitch into each stitch across the row.
- In the second chain, rotate your work from one side to the other. Then, again do a row of half double crochet stitches into each stitch across the row.
- Repeat these steps by rotating your work from one side to the other and changing between single and half double crochet stitches for the remainder of the blanket. This creates a simple single-crochet and half-double-crochet stitch pattern.
- Continue to work in the single crochet and half double crochet stitch pattern until the blanket reaches the desired length. The standard size for a baby blanket is about 36 inches by 36 inches.
- To finish off the baby blanket, cut off the yarn and leave a long tail end of about 12 inches. Then, thread the tail end onto a tapestry needle and weave it through the remaining stitches, pulling tight to close the last row.
- Weave in all remaining ends using a tapestry needle.

And that's it! You have now crocheted a beautiful baby blanket using single-crochet and half-double-crochet stitches. You can create a variety of blankets using different variations of stitches and yarn color and type.

Ear Warmers

Ear warmers are perfect for keeping your ears cozy during chilly weather, along with being a practical and stylish accessory. As a crochet beginner, this project is an excellent opportunity to learn new techniques while creating a functional and fashionable item. The beauty

of ear warmers is that they can be customized to suit your personal style and preferences. You can experiment with various colors, stitch patterns, and embellishments to create a unique and personalized accessory that reflects individuality. Crocheting an ear warmer is a simple and fun project for beginners. So, follow along with this step-by-step tutorial on how to crochet an ear warmer:

Materials:

- Worsted weight yarn in any color (approx. 50-100g)
- Crochet hook (size H/5mm is recommended)
- Scissors
- Tapestry needle

Instructions:

- Make a slipknot and chain 9 stitches onto your crochet hook. Then, in the fourth chain from the hook, make a double crochet stitch; this will count as your first stitch.
- Then, stitch into each chain across the row, making a double crochet.

- In the second chain, rotate your work from one side to the other. Then into the second stitch from your crochet hook, make another double crochet stitch.
- Then, again stitch into each chain across the row using a double crochet stitch.
- Repeat these steps for the remainder of the ear warmer to create a simple pattern with double crochet stitches.
- Then, continue working in the double crochet stitch pattern until the ear warmer reaches the desired length. For a standardized adult-sized ear warmer, the length should be about 20 inches.
- Fold it in half to finish the ear warmer and sew the two ends together using a tapestry needle and the same yarn used to crochet it.
- Weave in all remaining ends using a tapestry needle.

And that's it! You have now crocheted yourself a beautiful ear warmer. You can experiment with different yarn colors and textures to create a variety of ear warmers to match your personal style.

Note: This is for a standard ear warmer size; you can always measure your head size using a tape measure and make the width of your project accordingly.

Crochet Pillow Cover

Crocheting a pillow cover is perfect for beginners who want to add a touch of handmade charm to their home decor. It is a practical and creative endeavor, and it also allows you to personalize your living space with a cozy and stylish accessory. The beauty of crocheted pillow covers is their versatility. You can choose from an array of stitch patterns, colors, and textures to match your home decor and personal style. Whether you prefer a classic look or a more modern design, the possibilities are endless. This project is perfect for helping you to enhance your crochet skills and allows you to practice techniques such as creating different stitch patterns, working in the round, and joining pieces

together. With each stitch, you will witness your pillow cover come to life, adding warmth and personality to any room. Crocheting a simple pillow cover is a great project for beginners. So follow along with this easy step-by-step tutorial on how to crochet a simple pillow cover:

Materials:

- Worsted weight yarn in any color (approx. 200-300g)
- Crochet hook (size H/5mm is recommended)
- Scissors
- Tapestry needle
- 16-inch square pillow insert

Instructions:

- Make a slipknot and chain 51 stitches. Then, into the third chain from your crochet hook, make a double crochet stitch which will count as your first stitch.
- Then, make a stitch into each chain across the row using double crochet.

- In the second chain, rotate your work from one side to the other.
- Then, make another stitch into the second stitch from your crochet hook using the double crochet stitch. And, repeat this stitch into each stitch till the end of your row.
- Repeat these steps till your pillow cover is completed, and you have created a simple double crochet pattern.
- Then, continue working in the double crochet stitch pattern until the pillow cover measures 16 inches in width.
- Fold the pillow cover in half, with the right sides facing each other.
- Lastly, finish your pillow cover by using a single crochet join that you have learned in the previous chapter. All you have to do is insert your crochet hook into the top loop of the other-sided stitch and yarn over, then draw through both created loops till you complete your single crochet stitch. Repeat this stitch till the end of the side.
- Repeat the joining step for the other side of the pillow cover.
- Turn the pillow cover right side out and insert the pillow insert.
- To finish the pillow cover, single crochet along the top edge, joining the two halves together. Weave in all remaining ends using a tapestry needle.

And that's it! You made yourself a beautiful crocheted pillow cover. Try using different stitches and creating a variety of textures in your pillow covers to match your personal preference.

Crochet Sweater

Crocheting a sweater may seem like a daunting task; however, with the right guidance and a beginner-friendly pattern, it's an achievable and rewarding project. The beauty of crocheting your sweater is the opportunity for customization. You can choose from a variety of yarn colors, stitch patterns, and sizes to create a sweater that perfectly suits your style and body shape. It's a chance to express your creativity and showcase your fashion sense. This project may require some patience

and practice; however, it is an excellent way to develop your crochet skills. You will gain experience in shaping, increasing, and decreasing stitches, as well as working with different stitch patterns and joining pieces together. The result will be a wearable masterpiece that you can proudly show off. Crocheting a sweater can be a bit more challenging for beginners, however by following this easy step-by-step tutorial, you can learn how to crochet a simple sweater:

Materials:

- Worsted weight yarn in any color (approx. 500-1000g)
- Crochet hook (size I/5.5mm is recommended)
- Scissors
- Tapestry needle

Instructions:

- Choose your sweater pattern and size. For beginners, it is recommended to start with a simple sweater pattern, such as a top-down raglan or a basic sweater that requires minimal shaping.

- Before you start, make a gauge swatch to ensure that your sweater will fit properly. To do this, crochet a small sample piece of about 4 inches by 4 inches using your chosen yarn and hook size. Measure the number of stitches and rows you made per inch and adjust your hook size if necessary to achieve the correct gauge.
- Then, start crocheting the sweater according to your chosen pattern, and make sure to follow the instructions carefully. Most crochet sweaters involve crocheting the body and sleeves separately and then joining them together.
- Pay extra attention to the shaping of the sweater, such as the neckline, armholes, and waist. You can use stitch markers to keep track of where you need to increase or decrease your stitches.
- Crochet any additional design details, such as pockets, ribbing, or buttons, as specified in the pattern.
- Once the sweater is complete, weave in all remaining ends using a tapestry needle.
- Try on the sweater and make any necessary adjustments. If the fit is too loose or too tight, you can adjust the hook size or make modifications to the pattern.

And that's it! You can now crochet a beautiful sweater. Remember, crocheting a sweater requires a bit more skill and patience; however, with practice and determination, you can create a beautiful garment that you will be proud to wear.

Conclusion

In conclusion, crochet is a wonderful and rewarding craft that is easy to learn and can provide a lifetime of enjoyment. With the help of this book, beginners can learn the basics of crochet, including how to choose the right materials, read patterns, and create a variety of stitches and projects. Crochet is a craft that has been enjoyed for generations and has become increasingly popular in recent years. It provides a wonderful outlet for creativity and self-expression, allowing individuals to create beautiful, one-of-a-kind pieces that can be treasured for years to come. This book provides a comprehensive guide to crochet for beginners, including step-by-step instructions and illustrations for all the basic stitches and tips and tricks for working with different types of yarn and tools. Beginners will learn to read crochet patterns and do various projects, from simple dishcloths and scarves to more complex items like blankets and sweaters.

One of the great things about crochet is that it can be easily adapted to suit different skill levels and styles. Beginners can start with simple projects and gradually work their way up to more challenging ones as they become more comfortable with the craft. Crochet also provides a great opportunity to experiment with different colors, textures, and patterns, allowing beginners to develop their own unique style and express their creativity.

Another benefit of crochet is its therapeutic qualities. Many people find crochet a relaxing and meditative activity that helps them de-stress and unwind. It can also be a great way to connect with others and build a sense of community, whether through joining a crochet group or gifting handmade items to friends and family.

In short, this book has provided a comprehensive introduction to the wonderful world of crochet, from the basics to more advanced techniques. It has offered encouragement and guidance to beginners as they explore this exciting and rewarding craft and has provided inspiration for creating beautiful and unique projects. With a little practice and patience, anyone can learn to crochet and enjoy the many benefits that this timeless craft has to offer.

References

Abby. (2020, May 2). What is a Yarn Swift and is it Necessary? A Beginner's Guide. Sew Homey. https://sewhomey.com/what-is-a-yarn-swift-and-is-it-necessary-a-beginners-guide/

Ashley. (2022). How To Make a Bobble Stitch Headband- Free Crochet Pattern. A Crafty Concept. https://www.acraftyconcept.com/boho-bobble-twist-headband/

Basic Crochet Stitches — Chain Stitch. (2017, August 1). MAKEetc. https://makeetc.com/blogs/knitting-and-crochet-tutorials/basic-crochet-stitches-chain-stitch

Bykaterina. (2018, November 5). "My Precious" Sweater — ByKaterina. https://by-katerina.com/my-precious-sweater/

Cagle, K. (2022a). Easy Crochet Scrunchies Pattern. Easy Crochet Patterns. https://easycrochet.com/crochet-hair-scrunchie-pattern/

Cagle, K. (2022b). The Many Types of Crochet. Easy Crochet Patterns. https://easycrochet.com/the-many-types-of-crochet/

Cagle, K. (2023a). How to Crochet a Scarf for Beginners. Easy Crochet Patterns. https://easycrochet.com/crochet-scarf-for-beginners/

Cagle, K. (2023b). How to Crochet: A Guide to Crocheting for Beginners. Easy Crochet. https://easycrochet.com/Crochet-For-Beginners/

Cagle, K. (2023c). Double Crochet Beanie Pattern. Easy Crochet Patterns. https://easycrochet.com/womens-crochet-circle-button-hat/

Cagle, K. (2023d). Beginner Easy Crochet Washcloth Pattern. Easy Crochet Patterns. https://easycrochet.com/beginner-crochet-washcloth-pattern/

Cagle, K. (2023e). Free & Easy Crochet Ear Warmer Pattern. Easy Crochet Patterns. https://easycrochet.com/chained-crochet-headband-pattern/

Cagle, K. (2023f). How to Crochet a Classic Granny Square Pattern for Beginners. Easy Crochet Patterns. https://easycrochet.com/how-to-crochet-a-classic-granny-square/

Coach, C. C. (2022). 17 Beginner Crochet Mistakes You Need To Avoid. Crochet Coach. https://crochetcoach.com/beginner-crochet/

Crochet Coach. (2020, April 8). Types of Crochet – Crochet Coach. https://crochetcoach.com/lessons/types-of-crochet/

Crochet Edges. (n.d.). http://www.how-to-crochet-instructions.com/crochet-edges.html

Cromwell, V. (2022). How To Tell Right Side Of Crochet – 5 Easy Tricks. Blue Star Crochet. https://bluestarcrochet.com/how-to-tell-right-side-crochet/

Diana. (2023, January 26). Key Parts of a Crochet Hook: What Artists Need to Know! — Adventures with Art. Adventures with Art. https://adventureswithart.com/key-parts-of-a-crochet-hook/

Do You Project Bag? (n.d.). Tika Bags. https://tikabags.com/ceci-et-cela/do-you-project-bag/

Doraexplored. (2022). The truth about left-handed crochet: The differences for left handed crocheters. Dora Does. https://doradoes.co.uk/2022/06/07/the-truth-about-left-handed-crochet-the-differences-for-left-handed-crocheters/

Eckman, E. (2020). Crochet Yarn Overs and Yarn Unders: What’s the Difference? Edie Eckman. https://www.edieeckman.com/2020/01/21/crochet-yarn-over-yarn-under/

Erika. (2020). Types of Stitch Markers. Don't Be Such a Square. https://www.dontbesuchasquare.com/types-of-stitch-markers/

Field, L. (2022). Crochet Hooks: Types, Sizes, and How to Choose the Best One. Skillshare Blog. https://www.skillshare.com/en/blog/crochet-hooks-types-sizes-and-how-to-choose-the-best-one/

Goodale, C. (2021). 10 Common Mistakes Crocheters Make and How to Avoid Them | E'Claire Makery. E'Claire Makery |. https://eclairemakery.com/10-common-mistakes-crocheters-make-and-how-to-avoid-them/

How to Crochet Stitch Variations | Yarnspirations. (n.d.). https://www.yarnspirations.com/how-to-stitch-crochet-variations.html

How to do the Blanket Stitch — Sarah's Hand Embroidery Tutorials. (n.d.). Sarah's Hand Embroidery Tutorials. https://www.embroidery.rocksea.org/stitch/blanket-stitch/blanket-stitch/

How to Join Knitted Pieces by Sewing with Backstitch dummies. (2016). Dummies. https://www.dummies.com/article/home-auto-hobbies/crafts/knitting-crocheting/how-to-join-knitted-pieces-by-sewing-with-backstitch-206577/

Jackofsky, E. (2020). Crocheting in the Round: A Step by Step Tutorial. The Spruce Crafts. https://www.thesprucecrafts.com/crocheting-in-the-round-979084

Kleivset, J. (2023, February 16). Simple Crochet Pillow Cover Pattern — EASY Crochet Pattern. Joy of Motion Crochet. https://joyofmotioncrochet.com/simple-crochet-pillow-cover-pattern/

L, T. (2021). How to Increase and Decrease in Crochet. TL Yarn Crafts. https://tlycblog.com/crochet-increase-and-decrease/

Mirella. (2022). How to make Pom Poms using the Clover Pom Pom maker. Mirella Moments. https://mirellamoments.com/how-to-make-a-pom-pom/

Needlecraft, C. (2019, August 19). Tool School: Swatch Ruler and Needle Gauge. Clover Needlecraft. https://blog.clover-usa.com/2019/08/19/tool-school-swatch-ruler-and-needle-gauge/

Nilsson, K. (2023). How to Block Your Knitting Projects (4+ Methods With Videos). Knitting Knowledge. https://knittingknowledge.com/knitting-guides/how-to-block-your-knitting/

Olga. (2023). How to Crochet a Baby Blanket Step by Step. My Crochet Space. https://mycrochetspace.com/baby-blanket-step-by-step/

Rhondda. (2022). Joining Techniques for Crochet. Oombawka Design Crochet. https://oombawkadesigncrochet.com/joining-techniques-for-crochet/

Skuse, B. (2021, December 21). How to add embroidery on crochet. Gathered. https://www.gathered.how/knitting-and-crochet/crochet/how-to-add-embroidery-on-crochet/

Solovay, A. (2019). Simple Shell Stitch Crochet Edging Free Pattern. The Spruce Crafts. https://www.thesprucecrafts.com/simple-shell-stitch-crochet-edging-pattern-978649

Solovay, A. (2020a). Crocheting the Basic V-Stitch. The Spruce Crafts. https://www.thesprucecrafts.com/how-to-crochet-the-basic-v-stitch-978519

Stearns, S. (2022b). How to Crochet a Magic Ring (Magic Circle Tutorial). Sarah Maker. https://sarahmaker.com/crochet-magic-ring/

Stearns, S. (2022c). How to Weave in the Ends in Crochet. Sarah Maker. https://sarahmaker.com/weave-in-ends-crochet/

Thadani, P. (2019). Front Loop Only (flo) or Back Loop Only (blo) Crochet. Stitches N Scraps. https://stitchesnscraps.com/front-loop-only-flo-back-loop-only-blo-crochet/

Vercillo, K. (2020). Basketweave Crochet Baby Blanket Pattern. The Spruce Crafts. https://www.thesprucecrafts.com/basketweave-crochet-baby-blanket-pattern-4143230

Printed in Great Britain
by Amazon